Presented to

EMELIA KELLY

For

CAMP LEGO & LET GO

Date

GOD BLESS YOU!

Pam Vogel - GROUP LEADER

Print ISBN 978-1-63058-873-1

eBook Editions:
Adobe Digital Edition (.epub) 978-1-63409-339-2
Kindle and MobiPocket Edition (.prc) 978-1-63409-340-8

Published by Barbour Books, an imprint of Barbour Publishing, Inc., P.O. Box 719, Uhrichsville, Ohio 44683, www.barbourbooks.com

Our mission is to publish and distribute inspirational products offering exceptional value and biblical encouragement to the masses.

Member of the
Evangelical Christian
Publishers Association

Printed in the United States of America.
D10005350 0416 DP

The Bible Promise Book®

DEVOTIONAL & BIBLE MEMORY PLAN

▶▶▶▶▶ **for Kids**

• • • • • • • • • • • •

JEAN FISCHER

BARBOUR BOOKS
An Imprint of Barbour Publishing, Inc.

CONTENTS

INTRODUCTION

You have so much going on—school, friends, sports, and family activities. There's not always time to sit and read. That's what makes this devotional and Bible memory plan a great idea! These short readings and memory verses will give you all of the wisdom you need before heading out to school or to play. *And* you'll be learning a lot about yourself and God in a short time!

Your word is a lamp to guide my feet and a light for my path.
PSALM 119:105 NLT

Chapter 1

• • • • • • • • • • • • • • • • •

FRIENDSHIP

▶▶ Best Friends Forever!

Who are your friends? Most likely, there are friends you have known for most of your life. You have new friends, too, kids you met when you entered a new grade in school or when you began a new activity. Friends come in all shapes, sizes, and colors. Some are acquaintances—kids you see every day at school but don't hang out with. Others are best friends—kids you spend a lot of time with and trust to always be there for you.

Jesus is the best Friend of all. Why? Because whoever you are and wherever you go, He goes with you. Jesus always loves and cares for you. When you invite Him into your heart, you are guaranteed that He will be your best Friend forever! You can trust Jesus with everything. He already has an amazing plan for your life, and He is eager to hang out with you every day while you watch His plan unfold.

Memory Verses

Let's take a look at some Bible promises
about friendship with Jesus and others.

"For I know the plans I have for you," declares the Lord, "plans
to prosper you and not to harm you, plans to give you hope and
a future."

Jeremiah 29:11 NIV

One who loves a pure heart and who speaks with grace will
have the king for a friend.

Proverbs 22:11 NIV

"For the LORD your God is living among you. He is a mighty
savior. He will take delight in you with gladness. With his love,
he will calm all your fears. He will rejoice over you with joyful
songs."

Zephaniah 3:17 NLT

A friend is always loyal, and a brother is born to help in time of need.

Proverbs 17:17 NLT

• • • • • •

Behold, I stand at the door, and knock: if any man hear my voice, and open the door, I will come in to him, and will sup with him, and he with me.

Revelation 3:20 KJV

• • • • • •

Two people are better off than one, for they can help each other succeed.

Ecclesiastes 4:9 NLT

Memory Plan

· · · · · · · · · · · · · · · · · · · ·

Why is it important to memorize Bible promises? Because having God's Word in your heart helps you to know how He wants you to live. Just as important, it draws you closer to Him. The more time you spend with God, the more you will trust Him as your friend.

Memorizing scripture does not have to be hard. In fact, it can be fun. Try this memory challenge with a group of your friends. Each of you choose a promise from this chapter and create a song about it. Then teach the song to your friends and ask them to sing it with you.

Tips:
- Choose a unique style for your song: hip-hop, rap, pop, country . . .
- Make the song short so it's easy to remember.
- Use the complete Bible verse and its reference in the chorus. For example:
  Chorus—
  Two people are better off than one,
  for they can help each other succeed.
  Ecclesiastes 4:9 NLT

CHAPTER 2

. . . .

ALL ABOUT ME

▶▶ Designer Made

Designer clothes and accessories are everywhere. You see them in the stores: designer jeans, shoes, purses, glasses, and cell phone covers. Maybe you own a few of these items, or maybe a designer label isn't important to you.

The brand of clothing you wear or the name printed on the label doesn't matter. But what does matter is that you are your own, unique you! After all, like a one-of-a-kind outfit made for a celebrity, you are one of a kind. There is no one exactly like you anywhere on earth.

Psalm 139 includes a thank-You to God for making you so wonderfully complex. It says that when He made you, His workmanship was marvelous. If you read Psalm 139, you will learn that God knew you even before He made you inside your mother's body. He had already planned every day and every moment of your life. You can think of it this way: God is the perfect designer, and you are His best creation. If you had a designer label, it would say *Amazing!* because that's what you are, an amazing masterpiece made by God.

Memory Verses

· · · · · · · · · · · · · · · · · · · ·

What does the Bible say about you?

You saw me before I was born. Every day of my life was recorded in your book. Every moment was laid out before a single day had passed.

Psalm 139:16 NLT

· · · · · ·

But to all who believed him and accepted him, he gave the right to become children of God.

John 1:12 NLT

· · · · · ·

Don't you realize that your body is the temple of the Holy Spirit, who lives in you and was given to you by God? You do not belong to yourself.

1 Corinthians 6:19 NLT

For God bought you with a high price. So you must honor God with your body.

1 Corinthians 6:20 NLT

• • • • • •

For we are God's handiwork, created in Christ Jesus to do good works, which God prepared in advance for us to do.

Ephesians 2:10 NIV

• • • • • •

I will praise thee; for I am fearfully and wonderfully made: marvellous are thy works; and that my soul knoweth right well.

Psalm 139:14 KJV

Memory Plan

Before you try to memorize the verses in this chapter,
think about them. Try making them personal by
making them about you. Here are some examples.

Because I accepted Jesus and believe in Him, I am a child of
God. (John 1:12)

My body is the temple of the Holy Spirit, who lives in me and
was given to me by God. I belong to God, and not to me.
(1 Corinthians 6:19)

Because I belong to God and He lives in me, I will honor Him
with my body. (1 Corinthians 6:20)

After you have applied a verse to your own life, it becomes
easier to memorize.

CHAPTER 3

• • • • • • • • • • • • • •

CHALLENGES

▶▶ A Secret Weapon

The Bible includes many stories about people who faced challenges head-on. One of them was a kid named David.

The Philistine army was at war with Israel. The Philistines had a secret weapon. His name was Goliath, a giant, ferocious man who stood over nine feet tall! The Israelite soldiers were terrified of Goliath's size and strength.

One day, David's dad sent him to the battlefield to check on his older brothers. When David heard Goliath shouting and threatening the Israelite soldiers, it made him angry. He decided to fight the big bully. David had no armor and only a slingshot and a stone, but he had a secret weapon: God was on his side. Courageously, David shouted at Goliath, "You come against me with sword and spear and javelin, but I come against you in the name of the Lord Almighty, the God of the armies of Israel" (1 Samuel 17:45 NIV). Then David put the stone in his slingshot. He aimed. He fired a perfect shot that knocked Goliath dead! The Israelite soldiers were saved thanks to David and his secret weapon—God.

How are you at facing challenges? If a giant challenge comes your way, remember: God is on your side.

Memory Verses

. . . .

Isn't it great knowing that God will
help whenever you need Him?

I can do all things through Christ which strengtheneth me.

Philippians 4:13 KJV

. . . . . .

"Be strong and courageous, and do the work. Do not be afraid
or discouraged, for the LORD God, my God, is with you. He
will not fail you or forsake you."

1 Chronicles 28:20 NIV

. . . . . .

"For I hold you by your right hand—I, the LORD your God.
And I say to you, 'Don't be afraid. I am here to help you.'"

Isaiah 41:13 NLT

God arms me with strength, and he makes my way perfect.

Psalm 18:32 NLT

• • • • • •

"So be strong and courageous! Do not be afraid and do not panic before them. For the LORD your God will personally go ahead of you. He will neither fail you nor abandon you."

Deuteronomy 31:6 NLT

• • • • • •

Have not I commanded thee? Be strong and of a good courage; be not afraid, neither be thou dismayed: for the LORD thy God is with thee whithersoever thou goest.

Joshua 1:9 KJV

Memory Plan

. . . .

Memorizing many scripture verses is a challenge. Will you face that challenge head-on, or will you walk away?

Make it fun with some friendly competition. Pair up with a friend, and see which of you can memorize all of the verses in this chapter in the shortest amount of time. Ready? Set? Go!

There are many different versions of the Bible. Some are easier to read and understand than others. This book uses the King James Version (KJV), the New International Version (NIV), and the New Living Translation (NLT). Try sampling different versions of the Bible until you find one you like. You might also find Bibles written especially for kids your age.

Think about It

· · · · · · · · · · · · · · · · · · · ·

How do you feel when you face a big challenge?

When facing a challenge, what do you usually do?

Name three ways the verses in this chapter can help when you face a challenge.

Why do you think it is important to memorize scripture verses?

Which scripture verse in this chapter is your favorite?

If you could meet David, what would you say to him?

CHAPTER 4

· · · · · · · · · · · · · ·

COURAGE

▶▶ Yes, You Can!

> *"911. What's your emergency?"*
> *"My house is burning down! Send the fire department!"*
> *"I'm sorry. I can't."*

Try to imagine a world in which everyone says, "I can't." Houses would burn down, hospitals would shut down, and vehicles would stop running. Eventually, everything in the world would stand still. The world runs on people saying, "Yes, I can!" and often that takes courage.

Can you think of a time when you were afraid to do something and you did it anyway? That's courage! Sometimes you only need a little bit of courage. For example, a little courage might get you onto that scary carnival ride that you have been avoiding all day. Other things take a lot of courage, fighting a serious illness, for example, or facing the loss of someone you love.

Whenever your mind tells you, *I can't*, then listen to your heart. Jesus lives there, and He says, "Yes, you can!"

Memory Verses

• • • • • • • • • • • • • • • • • • • •

When your head says, *I can't!*
remember these verses and say, "Yes, I can!"

"Be strong and very courageous. Be careful to obey all the law my servant Moses gave you; do not turn from it to the right or to the left, that you may be successful wherever you go."

Joshua 1:7 NIV

• • • • • •

"But as for you, be strong and courageous, for your work will be rewarded."

2 Chronicles 15:7 NLT

• • • • • •

Be on your guard; stand firm in the faith; be courageous; be strong.

1 Corinthians 16:13 NIV

Be of good courage, and he shall strengthen your heart, all ye that hope in the LORD.

Psalm 31:24 KJV

• • • • • •

"When you pass through the waters, I will be with you; and when you pass through the rivers, they will not sweep over you. When you walk through the fire, you will not be burned; the flames will not set you ablaze. For I am the LORD your God, the Holy One of Israel, your Savior."

Isaiah 43:2–3 NIV

• • • • • •

Put on the full armor of God, so that you can take your stand against the devil's schemes.

Ephesians 6:11 NIV

Memory Plan

When you have Bible verses stored in your memory, you can call them up whenever you need them. It's like putting on armor. It gives you a courage boost by providing you with some good, solid protection.

Try this memory trick. Write down one of the verses from this chapter and tape it to a door that you open and close a lot. Before you open the door, read the verse out loud, paying close attention to the words. Then, before you close the door, try to say the verse from memory. If you practice doing this every day, you will memorize scripture in no time!

CHAPTER 5

. . . .

PRAYER

▶▶ Can I Get an Amen?

Other than talking face-to-face, how do you communicate with your friends? Maybe you text or call them from your cell phone. You might video-chat, for free, with friends all over the world, and, of course, there is always that old standby, email. Can you think of some other ways that you and your friends communicate?

Communicating with God is unlike any other form of communication because God is unlike anyone or anything else. Technology isn't necessary to reach Him. Everyone has a direct line to God through prayer, and the only thing required is a sincere heart.

Although God knows exactly where you are and what you are doing all the time, He still wants to hear from you. Imagine just following your friends around all the time and having them act like you aren't there. If you don't talk to God, then that's how you treat Him.

Prayer is important. It strengthens your relationship with God and draws Him into your everyday life. Get into the habit of talking with Him all day long. He is your very best friend, and you can tell Him anything. God is never too busy to listen or help.

Memory Verses

• •

The Bible says this about prayer:

Evening, and morning, and at noon, will I pray, and cry aloud: and he shall hear my voice.

Psalm 55:17 KJV

• • • • • •

How gracious he will be when you cry for help! As soon as he hears, he will answer you.

Isaiah 30:19 NIV

• • • • • •

The LORD is close to all who call on him, yes, to all who call on him in truth.

Psalm 145:18 NLT

He shall call upon me, and I will answer him: I will be with him in trouble; I will deliver him, and honour him.

Psalm 91:15 KJV

· · · · · ·

"The eyes of the LORD watch over those who do right, and his ears are open to their prayers. But the LORD turns his face against those who do evil."

1 Peter 3:12 NLT

· · · · · ·

Never stop praying.

1 Thessalonians 5:17 NLT

Memory Plan

. . . .

Games can be a fun way to learn scripture. Many games can be adapted to help you memorize. Try this one based on "Simon Says." The idea is to ask players to say a specific verse in a certain way (whisper it, sing it, shout it, rap it, yodel it!).

Choose one verse from this chapter.

The leader says: "Simon says, 'Sing it!'"

Then everyone sings their own version of the verse.

Play continues with the leader giving commands. If the leader does not say, "Simon says," and a player follows the command, then that player is out.

Play continues until just one player is left.

Can you think of other games to help you memorize scripture?

CHAPTER 6

· · · · · · · · · · · · ·

FEAR

▶▶ Things That Go Bump in the Night

When you were little, maybe you were afraid of the dark. Maybe you are still afraid of the dark! Everyone is afraid of something. Fear is a part of being human. It is a signal that danger might be near. If you want to think of fear in a positive way, you can think of it as a warning sign.

When that warning signal, fear, sounds inside of you, what should you do? Will you run? Will you stand tall and fight? That depends on the situation. There is one thing you must do, though—trust God. This is what He says: "Don't be afraid, for I am with you. Don't be discouraged, for I am your God. I will strengthen you and help you. I will hold you up with my victorious right hand" (Isaiah 41:10 NLT). Imagine that, God holding you up with His big, powerful, yet gentle hand. Fear can never get in your way because God is always with you. He strengthens and helps you every day of your life.

Memory Verses

. . . .

Whenever you feel afraid,
use these verses to calm yourself down.

"Don't be afraid, for I am with you. Don't be discouraged, for
I am your God. I will strengthen you and help you. I will hold
you up with my victorious right hand."

Isaiah 41:10 NLT

. . . . . .

For God hath not given us the spirit of fear; but of power, and
of love, and of a sound mind.

2 Timothy 1:7 KJV

. . . . . .

When you lie down, you will not be afraid; when you lie down,
your sleep will be sweet.

Proverbs 3:24 NIV

He will cover you with his feathers. He will shelter you with his wings. His faithful promises are your armor and protection. Do not be afraid of the terrors of the night, nor the arrow that flies in the day.

Psalm 91:4–5 NLT

• • • • • •

When thou passest through the waters, I will be with thee; and through the rivers, they shall not overflow thee: when thou walkest through the fire, thou shalt not be burned; neither shall the flame kindle upon thee.

Isaiah 43:2 KJV

• • • • • •

So we can say with confidence, "The LORD is my helper, so I will have no fear. What can mere people do to me?"

Hebrews 13:6 NLT

Memory Plan

. . . .

Try one of these arts and crafts ideas to help you remember longer Bible verses.

First, choose one of the longer verses in this chapter. Draw a picture that will help you remember the verse. You could draw a picture that tells a story or you could just draw key ideas from the verse. For example, a story picture for Isaiah 43:2 might show a person walking through a dangerous place with Jesus. A key idea picture would show water, a river, fire, and Jesus. If you are crafty, try using the verse in a craft. Make a bracelet using the key words, embroider the verse on a cap or a pair of jeans, or write it on a dry-erase board. What other ways can you think of to use arts and crafts to memorize scripture?

Think about It

· · · · · · · · · · · · · · · · · · · ·

Name two situations when it is appropriate to run when you feel afraid.

Name two situations when it is right to face fear head-on.

What does it mean to trust God?

Why is it important to memorize the verses in this chapter?

If you could choose just one verse from this chapter to help you face fear, which would it be?

What advice would you give a younger sister or brother when they feel afraid?

CHAPTER 7

• • • • • • • • • • • • •

GRACE

▶▶ What Does Grace Mean?

Grace is one of those words with several different meanings. If you are a dancer, people might say you are "graceful," meaning that you move in a smooth, elegant way. If you have "social graces," it means you are always polite and use good manners in public. "Grace" is also a name for a short prayer said before a meal. But there is another kind of grace, one much better than any other—God's grace.

God's grace means that He gives people wonderful blessings in life, much more than they deserve. The best example of God's grace is Jesus. His death on the cross gives people the gift of eternal life. If you believe in Him and ask Him to come into your heart, then someday you will live in heaven. That's grace: God showing His kindness to you not only now, but forever.

Think about the many ways God has blessed your life. Can you name at least five? When you pray, remember to thank God for His grace.

Memory Verses

· · · · · · · · · · · · · · · · · · · ·

When you read these Bible verses,
think about their meanings.

But unto every one of us is given grace according to the
measure of the gift of Christ.

Ephesians 4:7 KJV

· · · · · ·

God saved you by his grace when you believed. And you can't
take credit for this; it is a gift from God. Salvation is not a
reward for the good things we have done, so none of us can
boast about it.

Ephesians 2:8–9 NLT

· · · · · ·

And the child grew and became strong; he was filled with
wisdom, and the grace of God was on him.

Luke 2:40 NIV

Each time he said, "My grace is all you need. My power works best in weakness." So now I am glad to boast about my weaknesses, so that the power of Christ can work through me.

2 Corinthians 12:9 NLT

• • • • • •

The LORD is my shepherd; I shall not want.

Psalm 23:1 KJV

• • • • • •

May he grant your heart's desires and make all your plans succeed.

Psalm 20:4 NLT

Memory Plan

. . . .

Try this Bible memory activity for a rainy day or anytime you are stuck indoors.

Choose a verse from this chapter and write each word on an index card or a separate scrap of paper. Mix them up and put them in order. Then try this: Write the words for all six passages on separate cards. Mix them all together and see how long it takes you to put them in the correct order. Can you do it? It's not as easy as you might think. The first time you try, use the verses in the book to help you. Then try it again, this time using just your memory.

CHAPTER 8

• • • • • • • • • • • • •

FAITH

▶▶ Growing by Leaps and Bounds

If you were standing on the edge of a cliff and someone told you to jump, would you do it? Would you leap off that cliff if you were absolutely, positively sure that you would land safe and sound? To jump would mean taking a big leap of faith. You would jump off that cliff only because you were certain you would land safely.

When you have faith in—trust in—Jesus, you take a leap of faith. You can be absolutely certain that whatever danger you face, you will be okay because Jesus loves you. He is always with you no matter what. Jesus' plans for you are good ones, and when you put your faith in Him, you know that He will do whatever is best for you. Faith in Jesus is like having a soft place to fall.

Putting faith into action—trusting Jesus—is what helps you grow as a Christian. Are you facing a problem today? Is there something you are afraid of? Then say a prayer and ask Jesus to help you. Put all of your trust in Him.

Memory Verses

....

Have faith and put it into action by
remembering what the Bible says:

Now faith is the substance of things hoped for, the evidence of
things not seen.

Hebrews 11:1 KJV

......

"He will protect his faithful ones, but the wicked will disappear
in darkness. No one will succeed by strength alone."

1 Samuel 2:9 NLT

......

We are made right with God by placing our faith in Jesus
Christ. And this is true for everyone who believes, no matter
who we are.

Romans 3:22 NLT

He replied, "If you have faith as small as a mustard seed, you can say to this mulberry tree, 'Be uprooted and planted in the sea,' and it will obey you."

Luke 17:6 NIV

• • • • • •

In the same way, faith by itself, if it is not accompanied by action, is dead.

James 2:17 NIV

• • • • • •

For ye are all the children of God by faith in Christ Jesus.

Galatians 3:26 KJV

Memory Plan

· · · · · · · · · · · · · · · · · ·

This memory ball toss game can be played with just one friend or with many. If playing with just one, stand across from each other; if playing with many, stand in a circle.

One player has the ball and recites a Bible verse from memory. The player then tosses the ball to a friend and that friend must respond with the chapter and verse. For example:

Player 1: "Now faith is the substance of things hoped for, the evidence of things not seen."

Player 2: "Hebrews 11:1."

Player 2 then recites a verse and tosses the ball to another player. See how long you can play before someone misses. You can use Bible verses from any chapter in this book.

CHAPTER 9

• • • • • • • • • • • • •

PATIENCE

▶▶ Not Right Now

Think about how much you have grown in patience. When you were a little baby, you had no idea what patience meant. When you wanted something, you cried until you got it. But when you were old enough to understand, you learned that you can't always have what you want *right now*. You learned that patience means waiting, and not only waiting but also waiting with a good attitude.

The Bible includes a whole book written about a man named Job. He had lost everything. His family, crops, health, *everything* had been taken away from him. But Job trusted God. He patiently waited for God to make things better. And God did!

God wants you to be like Job, waiting patiently and trusting Him to act. It might take years for God to work out His plan for you. Waiting is hard, and God understands that. So when you feel impatient and are ready to give up, pray and ask God to help you have patience. He has good plans for you, but you need to remember that God doesn't always act right now. He acts when the time is just right. And God's timing is always perfect.

Memory Verses

....

Remember these verses when you feel impatient:

But let patience have her perfect work, that ye may be perfect and entire, wanting nothing.

James 1:4 KJV

......

The LORD is good unto them that wait for him, to the soul that seeketh him.

Lamentations 3:25 KJV

......

But they that wait upon the LORD shall renew their strength; they shall mount up with wings as eagles; they shall run, and not be weary; and they shall walk, and not faint.

Isaiah 40:31 KJV

Patient endurance is what you need now, so that you will continue to do God's will. Then you will receive all that he has promised.

Hebrews 10:36 NLT

• • • • • •

We do not want you to become lazy, but to imitate those who through faith and patience inherit what has been promised.

Hebrews 6:12 NIV

• • • • • •

But if we hope for what we do not yet have, we wait for it patiently.

Romans 8:25 NIV

Memory Plan

• • • • • • • • • • • • • • • • •

When you pray, God loves it if you quote scripture verses to Him. It shows Him that you are interested in what He has to say and that you trust Him to act on His promises.

Try this. Memorize one of the verses in this chapter and then use it in a prayer. Here is an example using Hebrews 10:36 (NLT):

Dear God, the Bible says: "Patient endurance is what you need now, so that you will continue to do God's will. Then you will receive all that he has promised." I want to be patient and do what You want, but being patient is hard sometimes. Please help me to be patient and wait. I believe You are working out Your plan for me just like You promised. Amen.

Think about It

• •

Do you think you could be as patient and trusting as Job was?

What makes you feel impatient?

Why do you think patience is important?

Name one time when you waited patiently with a good attitude.

Why do you think God might make you wait awhile for what you want?

Which memory verse in this chapter do you like best? Why?

CHAPTER 10

• • • • • • • • • • • • •

CHILDREN'S DUTIES

▶▶ Make Jesus (and Your Parents) Proud!

The Bible tells about a time when Jesus was in the middle of a huge crowd. People followed Him wherever He went because they knew that Jesus could do amazing things. He was able to heal the sick, and He had many wise things to say.

Some parents wanted Jesus to bless their children and pray for them, so they tried to push their way through the crowd to get to Him. But when Jesus' disciples saw them, they told the parents and kids to stop.

"Don't bother Jesus!" they said.

Jesus didn't like that one bit. He said to His disciples, "Let the children come to Me. Don't stop them!" Then Jesus held the children, and He blessed them.

Jesus loves kids. He wants children to come to Him. He even assigns special duties to help kids grow up to be strong Christian adults. Those duties include things like being respectful, making good choices, and doing what is right.

Can you think of other good ways to behave? When you behave well, you make Jesus and your parents proud.

Memory Verses

• •

These verses will help you know
what God expects from you:

Children, always obey your parents, for this pleases the Lord.

Colossians 3:20 NLT

• • • • • •

"Honor your father and mother, as the LORD your God
commanded you. Then you will live a long, full life in the land
the LORD your God is giving you."

Deuteronomy 5:16 NLT

• • • • • •

My son, obey your father's commands, and don't neglect your
mother's instruction.

Proverbs 6:20 NLT

A wise son brings joy to his father, but a foolish son brings grief to his mother.

Proverbs 10:1 NIV

• • • • • •

Even a child is known by his doings, whether his work be pure, and whether it be right.

Proverbs 20:11 KJV

• • • • • •

My son, give me your heart and let your eyes delight in my ways.

Proverbs 23:26 NIV

Memory Plan

Each day this week, choose and memorize one of the Bible verses in this chapter. Then put that verse into action. Can you do what it says, all day long?

Colossians 3:20: Do whatever your parents ask of you.

Deuteronomy 5:16: Find special ways to show respect to your parents.

Proverbs 6:20: Obey your mom and dad—all day long.

Proverbs 10:1: Learn something new today. Then tell your parents about what you learned. Remember to share this verse with them, too.

Proverbs 20:11: Do good works today without being asked. Help your mom and dad around the house.

Think about what you did this week. Did you put all the scripture verses into action? Did you please Jesus and your parents?

CHAPTER 11

· · · · · · · · · · · · · · · ·

GUILT/GOD'S FORGIVENESS

▶▶ Not Guilty!

Austin decided that his little sister was a pest. Whenever he wanted to play with his friends, she wanted to play, too. It finally made Austin so mad that he turned to her and said, "Go away! Find someone your own age to play with." As soon as he said it, Austin felt guilty. He knew that he had hurt his sister's feelings.

Do you feel guilty when you do something wrong? Guilt is God's way of telling you that He is not pleased by your behavior. But you can make things right again. The Bible says that if you confess your sins to God, He will forgive you. He will wipe away your sin and say, "Not guilty!"

Austin prayed and told God that he was sorry for speaking unkindly to his sister. He asked God's forgiveness. Then Austin went to his sister and asked her to forgive him, too.

Everyone messes up sometimes. When guilt reminds you that you have messed up, then make things right. Ask God, and others, to forgive you.

Memory Verses

. . . .

Memorize these verses to remind you that
God is good and that He forgives you.

I write unto you, little children, because your sins are forgiven
you for his name's sake.

1 John 2:12 KJV

. . . . . .

If we confess our sins, he is faithful and just to forgive us our
sins, and to cleanse us from all unrighteousness.

1 John 1:9 KJV

. . . . . .

Even if we feel guilty, God is greater than our feelings, and he
knows everything.

1 John 3:20 NLT

"For I will forgive their wickedness and will remember their sins no more."

Jeremiah 31:34 NIV

• • • • • •

Let the wicked change their ways and banish the very thought of doing wrong. Let them turn to the LORD that he may have mercy on them. Yes, turn to our God, for he will forgive generously.

Isaiah 55:7 NLT

• • • • • •

"For I will forgive their wickedness and will remember their sins no more."

Hebrews 8:12 NIV

Memory Plan

• • • • • • • • • • • • • • • • •

Have fun play-acting this game with three friends. Each of you will play a part. You will need a prosecutor, a defense attorney, a judge, and a person accused of a crime. Make up silly crimes like stealing the noodles from the soup or whistling in your bedroom after midnight. Play goes like this:

PROSECUTOR: "You have been found guilty of [make up something funny]."

GUILTY PERSON: "I confess that I did it, and I'm sorry."

DEFENSE ATTORNEY: "The Bible says: [Quote one of the memory verses from this chapter.]"

JUDGE: "The Bible is always right. So I find you not guilty!"

Take turns switching roles so everyone has a chance to say a verse.

CHAPTER 12

· · · · · · · · · · · · · ·

FORGIVING OTHERS

▶▶ We All Mess Up

Humans are, well—human! None of us is perfect. The only One who is and ever was perfect is Jesus. He was God come to earth in a human body. Jesus always did what was right. He never messed up, but every other person who has ever lived has made mistakes.

Think about all the people you know. They make mistakes sometimes, right? You make mistakes, too. Jesus knows that people are imperfect, and when they mess up He wants them to forgive one another. After all, He always forgives you. You learned about that in the last chapter. Now it is your turn to be like Jesus and forgive others.

Forgiveness isn't always easy. Sometimes people are not sorry for what they did. Jesus wants you to forgive them anyway. You can do that by forgiving them in your heart. You can also pray for them and ask Jesus to help them do what is right.

Is there someone you need to forgive today? Jesus will help you to do that.

Memory Verses

. . . .

This is what the Bible says about forgiving others.

"For if you forgive other people when they sin against you, your heavenly Father will also forgive you."

Matthew 6:14 NIV

. . . . . .

But I say unto you, Love your enemies, bless them that curse you, do good to them that hate you, and pray for them which despitefully use you, and persecute you.

Matthew 5:44 KJV

. . . . . .

"But love your enemies, do good to them, and lend to them without expecting to get anything back. Then your reward will be great, and you will be children of the Most High."

Luke 6:35 NIV

Get rid of all bitterness, rage and anger, brawling and slander, along with every form of malice. Be kind and compassionate to one another, forgiving each other, just as in Christ God forgave you.

Ephesians 4:31–32 NIV

• • • • • •

Then Peter came to Jesus and asked, "Lord, how many times shall I forgive my brother or sister who he sins against me? Up to seven times?" Jesus answered, "I tell you, not seven times, but seventy-seven times."

Matthew 18:21–22 NIV

• • • • • •

Judge not, and ye shall not be judged: condemn not, and ye shall not be condemned: forgive, and ye shall be forgiven.

Luke 6:37 KJV

Memory Plan

. . . .

When you memorize scripture, make sure you
get the words right. Leaving out just one little
word can change the entire meaning of a verse.
Which of these verses is correct?

Judge not, and ye shall be judged: condemn, and ye shall not be
condemned: forgive, and ye shall be forgiven.

Luke 6:37 KJV

Judge not, and ye shall not be judged: condemn not, and ye
shall not be condemned: forgive, and ye shall be forgiven.

Luke 6:37 KJV

What word is missing from the incorrect verse?

Think about It

· · · · · · · · · · · · · · · · · ·

Why is Jesus perfect?

Name a time when someone forgave you. How did it make you feel?

Why is it important to forgive others?

How can the memory verses in this chapter help you to be more forgiving?

Is there someone you need to forgive?

When you mess up, who will always forgive you?

CHAPTER 13

· · · · · · · · · · · · · ·

TRUST

▶▶ Just Do It!

Do you remember the story of Noah?

It so broke God's heart that His world was full of evil people that He decided to perform a do-over. God planned a great flood to cover the earth and destroy every living thing. That's where Noah comes in. He was the only good guy left on earth.

God told Noah to build a huge boat and fill it up with pairs of every kind of animal. God said something like, "Trust Me, Noah. I'm going to destroy everything on the earth. But your family, your boat, and everything in it will be safe."

If God told you to build a boat and load it with your family and a bunch of stinky animals, would you do it? As crazy as the boat idea sounded, Noah trusted God, and God did exactly what He promised. He saved Noah, his family, and the animals from the great flood.

The Bible is full of God's promises, and you can trust every one of them because God always does exactly what He says. Noah believed that, and you should, too.

When God promises to do something, trust Him. Just do it!

Memory Verses

....

God is trustworthy all the time.
Remember that by memorizing these verses:

Trust in the LORD with all thine heart; and lean not unto thine
own understanding. In all thy ways acknowledge him, and he
shall direct thy paths.

Proverbs 3:5–6 KJV

......

Blessed is that man that maketh the LORD his trust.

Psalm 40:4 KJV

......

Commit everything you do to the LORD. Trust him, and he will
help you.

Psalm 37:5 NLT

The LORD is my strength and shield. I trust him with all my heart. He helps me, and my heart is filled with joy. I burst out in songs of thanksgiving.

Psalm 28:7 NLT

• • • • • •

"But blessed are those who trust in the LORD and have made the LORD their hope and confidence. They are like trees planted along a riverbank, with roots that reach deep into the water. Such trees are not bothered by the heat or worried by long months of drought. Their leaves stay green, and they never stop producing fruit."

Jeremiah 17:7–8 NLT

• • • • • •

Fear of man will prove to be a snare, but whoever trusts in the LORD is kept safe.

Proverbs 29:25 NIV

Memory Plan

· · · · · · · · · · · · · · · · · · ·

When memorizing long Bible promises, it helps to memorize them in short sections. For example, when memorizing Jeremiah 17:7–8 (NLT), first learn the first part:

But blessed are those who trust in the LORD and have made the LORD their hope and confidence.

When you know the first part, then memorize the middle part:

They are like trees planted along a riverbank, with roots that reach deep into the water. Such trees are not bothered by the heat or worried by long months of drought.

And then learn the last part:

Their leaves stay green, and they never stop producing fruit.

Finally, put it all together:

But blessed are those who trust in the LORD and have made the LORD their hope and confidence. They are like trees planted along a riverbank, with roots that reach deep into the water. Such trees are not bothered by the heat or worried by long months of drought. Their leaves stay green, and they never stop producing fruit.

Memorizing long verses this way makes them easier to learn.

CHAPTER 14

· · · · · · · · · · · · · ·

ANGER

▶▶ I'm So Angry!

Sometimes God gets angry, but the Bible says He is slow to anger. God wants people to be slow to anger, too.

Those words "slow to anger" mean that you should stop and think whenever you get mad. Ask yourself whether you are right to be angry. Then decide what to do with your anger. Sometimes when people get mad, they shout or say and do things they don't mean. That's not what God wants. There are much better ways.

Sometimes walking away and calming down is the best thing to do. Calming down and thinking about why you are angry helps. If you were wrong to get angry, then after you calm down you can offer a sincere apology. If you still feel that you were right to be angry, then you can discuss it when you are calm and, hopefully, work things out. Often when you feel angry, after you are calm you will discover that the issue is so small that the best thing to do is forget about it and let it go.

Remember this: When you feel angry, God is watching you. He will help you know what to do.

Memory Verses

· ·

Here are some great verses to remember when you get angry.
Keep them close to your heart.

Fools vent their anger, but the wise quietly hold it back.

Proverbs 29:11 NLT

· · · · · ·

A gentle answer turns away wrath, but a harsh word stirs up
anger.

Proverbs 15:1 NIV

· · · · · ·

But now you must also rid yourselves of all such things as
these: anger, rage, malice, slander, and filthy language from
your lips.

Colossians 3:8 NIV

My dear brothers and sisters, take note of this: Everyone should be quick to listen, slow to speak and slow to become angry, because human anger does not produce the righteousness that God desires.

James 1:19–20 NIV

• • • • • •

And "don't sin by letting anger control you." Don't let the sun go down while you are still angry.

Ephesians 4:26 NLT

• • • • • •

The LORD is gracious, and full of compassion; slow to anger, and of great mercy.

Psalm 145:8 KJV

Memory Plan

Make a scripture memory poster for your bedroom using the verses in this chapter. Ask your parents whether you can put the poster on your wall someplace where you can easily see it from your bed. Use your poster to help you remember how God wants you to act when you feel angry.

Leave the poster up even after you have memorized the verses. Then it will always be there to remind you to handle your anger in a Christian way.

You might want to add a beautiful sunset to your poster to help you remember Ephesians 4:26—it's always good to get rid of your anger before you go to bed at night.

CHAPTER 15

• • • • • • • • • • • • • • •

GOD'S PEACE

▶▶ Perfect Peace

Quick. Name a peaceful place. Ready? Set? Go!

How did you answer? Maybe you said your backyard at night looking at the stars. Or maybe you've been to a farm in the country, away from all the city noise, and you found that to be peaceful.

Peace is a soft feeling. When you feel peaceful, you feel safe and know that everything is all right.

The apostle Paul wrote about peace. He said, "Don't worry about anything; instead, pray about everything. Tell God what you need, and thank him for all he has done. Then you will experience God's peace, which exceeds anything we can understand. His peace will guard your hearts and minds as you live in Christ Jesus" (Philippians 4:6–7 NLT).

Paul wrote those words while he suffered in a prison cell in Rome! The Romans had their own gods, so they put Paul in prison for preaching about his God, Jesus. But in the worst circumstances, Paul felt peace because he knew that Jesus was always with him.

Jesus is always with you, too. Peace comes by trusting Him and believing that He knows exactly how to make things right.

Memory Verses

•••••••••••••••••••••••

Use these verses to help you find
that soft feeling called "peace."

Don't worry about anything; instead, pray about everything.
Tell God what you need, and thank him for all he has done.
Then you will experience God's peace, which exceeds anything
we can understand. His peace will guard your hearts and minds
as you live in Christ Jesus.

Philippians 4:6–7 NLT

••••••

I will both lay me down in peace, and sleep: for thou, LORD,
only makest me dwell in safety.

Psalm 4:8 KJV

••••••

Now may the Lord of peace himself give you peace at all times
and in every way. The Lord be with all of you.

2 Thessalonians 3:16 NIV

For God is not a God of disorder but of peace.

1 Corinthians 14:33 NLT

· · · · · ·

"Don't be afraid," he said, "for you are very precious to God. Peace! Be encouraged! Be strong!"

Daniel 10:19 NLT

· · · · · ·

Peace I leave with you, my peace I give unto you: not as the world giveth, give I unto you. Let not your heart be troubled, neither let it be afraid.

John 14:27 KJV

Memory Plan

Ask your parents if you can go somewhere peaceful to memorize the verses in this chapter. Maybe you could make a tent in your house or yard. Pack up a lunch or some snacks, and have some quiet time alone to memorize the verses.

Remember to say a prayer, too. Paul told us how to pray. He said, "Tell God what you need, and thank him for all he has done. Then you will experience God's peace, which exceeds anything we can understand" (Philippians 4:6 NLT).

Think about It

. . . .

How would you describe peace?

God's peace is sometimes called "perfect peace." Why do you think His peace is perfect?

God's peace is also described as "everlasting." What do you think that means?

Name a situation in which you felt absolutely safe and peaceful.

Where did you go to memorize the verses in this chapter? Did you find it easier to memorize verses in a peaceful place?

When you need some soft-feeling peace, how might Jesus help you?

CHAPTER 16

• • • • • • • • • • • • • • •

PEACE WITH OTHERS

▶▶ Pass the Peace, Please

God doesn't want you to keep His peace all to yourself. He wants you to pass it on to others.

One way to share God's peace is by being peaceful toward everyone. You have already learned much about peace through these chapters. You've learned to show peace by being patient with others. You've learned to show it by doing what your parents ask without arguing with them. You've learned to pass God's peace to others whenever you forgive someone or when you hold back your anger. See? You already know how to pass the peace.

Jesus is the perfect example of peace. Even when people treated Him badly, Jesus reacted peacefully. He had all the power to smash those people like bugs! But Jesus didn't do that. He spoke words that were wise, yet gentle. He didn't get mad and yell at people. He forgave them—always—even when they nailed Him to the cross.

Think of the ways you have shared God's peace today. What can you do tomorrow to show even more peace toward others?

Memory Verses

The Bible says this about sharing God's peace:

Blessed are the peacemakers: for they shall be called the children of God.

Matthew 5:9 KJV

If it is possible, as far as it depends on you, live at peace with everyone.

Romans 12:18 NIV

Depart from evil, and do good; seek peace, and pursue it.

Psalm 34:14 KJV

Her ways are ways of pleasantness, and all her paths are peace.

Proverbs 3:17 KJV

• • • • • •

Better a dry crust eaten in peace than a house filled with feasting—and conflict.

Proverbs 17:1 NLT

• • • • • •

And those who are peacemakers will plant seeds of peace and reap a harvest of righteousness.

James 3:18 NLT

Memory Plan

• • • • • • • • • • • • • • • • • •

After you have memorized the verses in this chapter, see if you can find ways to share them with others. You could write a verse in a card and give it to someone, or you could make them a picture showing how the verse could be put into action. You might also recite the verses from memory to a grandparent or other adult. What other ways can you think of to share God's peace?

CHAPTER 17

· · · · · · · · · · · · ·

JUDGING OTHERS

▶▶ Bullies

Do you know any bullies? Most kids do. Bullies are mean to other kids. They make fun of them and judge them for the ways they look, act, or talk, whom they hang out with, and for so many other things. Bullies find plenty of reasons to judge people—and all of them are wrong.

Bullies usually put their thoughts into action. They judge others and they punish them, too. But there is another kind of bully: the silent bully. The silent bully unfairly judges people on the inside but doesn't show it on the outside.

In God's eyes, bullies are bullies. Jesus said we should not be unfair when judging others. Judgment belongs to God in heaven and to judges who preside over courts here on earth. Our job is to know right from wrong, to pray for the bullies, and to do our very best to get along with everyone all the time.

Stop right now and say a prayer for a bully you know. Ask God to help him or her to be kind like Jesus.

Memory Verses

· ·

Everyone judges others sometimes. It is part of being human.
These verses will remind you not to judge unfairly.

"Do not judge, or you too will be judged. For in the same way
you judge others, you will be judged, and with the measure you
use, it will be measured to you."

Matthew 7:1–2 NIV

· · · · · ·

"And why worry about a speck in your friend's eye when you
have a log in your own?"

Matthew 7:3 NLT

· · · · · ·

"How can you think of saying to your friend, 'Let me help you
get rid of that speck in your eye,' when you can't see past the
log in your own eye?"

Matthew 7:4 NLT

Judge not according to the appearance, but judge righteous judgment.

John 7:24 KJV

● ● ● ● ● ●

When they kept on questioning [Jesus], he straightened up and said to them, "Let any one of you who is without sin be the first to throw a stone at her."

John 8:7 NIV

● ● ● ● ● ●

There is one lawgiver, who is able to save and to destroy: who art thou that judgest another?

James 4:12 KJV

Memory Plan

● ● ● ● ● ● ● ● ● ● ● ● ● ● ● ● ● ●

Ask your parents if you can have some old newspapers. Choose one of the scripture verses in this chapter and see if you can find and cut out all of the words in the verse. Put the cut-out words in order. Can you do it from memory? Can you do it for all of the verses?

CHAPTER 18

· · · · · · · · · · · · ·

THE WORLD

▶▶ What in the World!

The world is a beautiful place with mountains to climb, oceans to sail on, caverns to explore, and woodlands to hike in. The world is full of amazing plants and animals. And every day there are stories of good people doing good things.

But the world is sometimes a scary place. That is because evil lives alongside good on earth. That's how it has been since Adam and Eve were kicked out of the garden of Eden. Bad things happen, and some people do bad things. That is just how it is.

The good news—the very best news—is that God has never, ever left His world. He is always here watching. He watches all the good things and the bad things, too. And one day, God will judge all of the world's people. Those who believe in Him will be taken up to heaven to live with Him. And those who don't believe? Well, they will be left behind.

God loves the world, and He loves you, too. So whenever the world seems scary and you wonder what in the world is happening, don't worry! God is watching, and He will take care of you.

Memory Verses

· ·

Memorize these verses and remember—God is more powerful than anything in the world, and He is in charge.

For God so loved the world, that he gave his only begotten Son, that whosoever believeth in him should not perish, but have everlasting life.

John 3:16 KJV

· · · · · ·

But you belong to God, my dear children. You have already won a victory over those people, because the Spirit who lives in you is greater than the spirit who lives in the world.

1 John 4:4 NLT

· · · · · ·

The earth is the LORD's, and everything in it, the world, and all who live in it.

Psalm 24:1 NIV

For God sent not his Son into the world to condemn the world; but that the world through him might be saved.

John 3:17 KJV

• • • • • •

Let all creation rejoice before the LORD, for he comes, he comes to judge the earth. He will judge the world in righteousness and the peoples in his faithfulness.

Psalm 96:13 NIV

• • • • • •

"I have told you all this so that you may have peace in me. Here on earth you will have many trials and sorrows. But take heart, because I have overcome the world."

John 16:33 NLT

Memory Plan

Sometimes it is easier to memorize a verse
by first asking yourself a question and then
reciting the answer verse. For example,

Question: Why did God send Jesus into the world?
Answer: John 3:16

Question: To whom do you belong?
Answer: 1 John 4:4

Question: To whom does the world and everything in it
belong?
Answer: Psalm 24:1

Can you come up with your own questions for the last three
memory verses in this chapter?

Think about It

....

Can you name three good-news stories you have heard this week?

How do the verses you memorized this week help you feel safe in the world?

Who judges the world and all its nations?

What can you do to promote good news in your school and community?

What should you do when you hear bad news or news that is scary?

In this changing world, why do you think it is so important to remember what God says in the Bible?

CHAPTER 19

. . . .

GOD'S LOVE FOR US

▶▶ Squeaky Clean

When God saw people giving in to evil, He did a do-over. He used the flood to wash the earth clean and started again hoping that people would behave. But they didn't. They kept on disobeying God and doing bad things.

God could have just said, "Enough of this!" and left the earth alone or destroyed it altogether. But He didn't. Instead, He made a way for people to be saved from evil. God sent His Son, Jesus, to accept the punishment for all the people's sins—all the people who lived then and would ever live on earth. God loves His children so much that if they believe that Jesus died for their sins, they are guaranteed a place in heaven when *they* die.

Everyone sins because they are human. Jesus is the only One who is perfect. God knows that people sin, and there is no place for sin in heaven. So through Jesus, God washes away our sin. He makes us squeaky clean to live with Him in heaven someday. That's how much He loves us!

God loves you because you are His. He loves you no matter what you do, and He will love you forever.

Memory Verses

. . . .

Remember—God loves you right now and forever!
The Bible tells you so:

But God demonstrates his own love for us in this: While we
were still sinners, Christ died for us.

Romans 5:8 NIV

. . . . . .

We know how much God loves us, and we have put our trust
in his love. God is love, and all who live in love live in God,
and God lives in them.

1 John 4:16 NLT

. . . . . .

See how very much our Father loves us, for he calls us his
children, and that is what we are! But the people who belong to
this world don't recognize that we are God's children because
they don't know him.

1 John 3:1 NLT

For as high as the heavens are above the earth, so great is his love for those who fear him.

Psalm 103:11 NIV

• • • • • •

No power in the sky above or in the earth below—indeed, nothing in all creation will ever be able to separate us from the love of God that is revealed in Christ Jesus our Lord.

Romans 8:39 NLT

• • • • • •

Give thanks to the LORD, for he is good. His love endures forever.

Psalm 136:1 NIV

Memory Plan

. . . .

First, memorize the promise verses in this chapter and think about them. Then be on the lookout this week for "God sightings." A God sighting is when you see God's love at work in your life. Maybe you were about to do or say something you shouldn't, and God reminded you not to. That's a God sighting. Or maybe God allowed something really special to happen to you this week. That's a God sighting, too!

Make a list of all your God sightings. Look hard. How long of a list can you make?

CHAPTER 20

• • • • • • • • • • • • • • •

WORSHIP/LOVING GOD

▶▶ Thank God!

God must really, *really* love you! After all, He follows you around all the time watching out for you. He reminds you inside your heart to do what is right and good. Best of all, He made you and He has a wonderful plan for your life. So how can you thank Him for blessing you like that? How can you love Him back?

The answer is simple—worship. The word *worship* means showing God through words and actions that you think He is awesome. You worship God in prayer by telling Him that you love Him instead of just asking Him for stuff. You worship God by singing praise songs to Him. You can also worship Him by looking for all the small things He does for you every day and saying thank You: *Thank You, God, for waking me up this morning. Thank You, God, for colors. Thank You for butterflies and music and for family and friends . . .* There are endless things to thank Him for.

Take a minute, right now, to bow your head and tell God that you love Him. Hearing from you will make Him glad.

Memory Verses

. . . .

Memorize these verses because you love
God and want to learn about Him.

Worship the Lord with gladness; come before him with joyful
songs.

Psalm 100:2 NIV

. . . . . .

And thou shalt love the Lord thy God with all thine heart,
and with all thy soul, and with all thy might.

Deuteronomy 6:5 KJV

. . . . . .

O come, let us worship and bow down: let us kneel before the
Lord our maker.

Psalm 95:6 KJV

You alone are the Lord. You made the skies and the heavens and all the stars. You made the earth and the seas and everything in them. You preserve them all, and the angels of heaven worship you.

Nehemiah 9:6 NLT

• • • • • •

Give unto the Lord the glory due unto his name; worship the Lord in the beauty of holiness.

Psalm 29:2 KJV

• • • • • •

Jesus answered, "It is written: 'Worship the Lord your God and serve him only.'"

Luke 4:8 NIV

Memory Plan

. . . .

Memorizing Bible verses is an excellent way to show God that you love Him. When you take time to learn about God, it pleases Him. When you know His words from the Bible by heart, it brings God even nearer to you. Learning Bible verses might seem like homework sometimes, but it is important to remember what God has to say; then you can live a fruitful Christian life by following His instructions. Ask God to be your Bible-memory Helper. Write a poem or a letter to Him telling Him why you love Him.

CHAPTER 21

· · · · · · · · · · · · ·

LOVING OTHERS

▶▶ Sharing God's Love

There are some people in your life to whom you say, "I love you." Your family members, for example. Those three little words—*I love you*—can make you, and just about everyone else, feel awesome. When you feel loved, you feel good about yourself.

But love is more than words. True love means *showing* God's love to everybody.

God wants us to build each other up by loving one another. There are many ways to show God's love. You can love others by donating to a food bank. You can show love to a new kid at school by being their friend. You can be kind and helpful wherever you go.

Jesus said, "Love each other in the same way that I have loved you." Read your Bible and learn all you can about Jesus. While you read, think about the ways He showed love to others. Jesus didn't go around saying, "I love you," to everybody. Instead, He did things to *show* others that they were loved.

What ways can you think of to share God's love?

Memory Verses

· ·

The Bible says this about love:

This is my commandment, That ye love one another, as I have loved you.

John 15:12 KJV

· · · · · ·

Love is patient and kind. Love is not jealous or boastful or proud or rude.

1 Corinthians 13:4–5 NLT

· · · · · ·

[Love] does not demand its own way. It is not irritable, and it keeps no record of being wronged.

1 Corinthians 13:5 NLT

[Love] does not rejoice about injustice but rejoices whenever the truth wins out.

1 Corinthians 13:6 NLT

• • • • • •

Love never gives up, never loses faith, is always hopeful, and endures through every circumstance.

1 Corinthians 13:7 NLT

• • • • • •

Dear children, let us not love with words or speech but with actions and in truth.

1 John 3:18 NIV

Memory Plan

. . . .

Invite some friends over and memorize the verses in this chapter together. Then think of ways that all of you can put the Bible verses into action. You might want to start a "Love One Another" club and put love into action in your community. Ask your parents or church youth pastor for ideas about ways that you can help others by sharing God's love.

Think about It

. . . .

How would you define love?

Who loves you? How do you know that they love you?

Whom do you love?

Why should you memorize the love verses in this chapter?

Why is it important to show others that God loves them?

What does it mean to love in actions and in truth?

CHAPTER 22

· · · · · · · · · · · · ·

SPEECH/WORDS

▶▶ What Did You Say?

Words are important because they have power. Soft, gentle words bring comfort, and kind, encouraging words help people feel good about themselves. Harsh words do just the opposite. They make people uncomfortable and tear people down.

God dislikes words that are not right and true. In the Bible story about the Tower of Babel, when the people made God angry He changed one language into many different languages so the people could not understand one another (Genesis 11:1–9). And Luke 1:5–25 tells about Zechariah, who did not believe in something God promised to do. So God punished him by taking away his voice for a while.

You should always be careful with the words you say. Use them in a way that pleases God. Mean words and swear words have no place in God's world. And the Ten Commandments tell us never to use God's or Jesus' name in vain (Exodus 20:7). That means you should never swear using God's name or even say things like "Oh my God." His name should always be used with respect.

Be careful what you say. Before words leave your lips, ask yourself: *Will God approve of my words?*

Memory Verses

....

Think of each verse while you memorize it. Are you guilty of using bad language? If you are, ask God to forgive you. He promises that He will.

Thou shalt not take the name of the LORD thy God in vain; for the LORD will not hold him guiltless that taketh his name in vain.

Exodus 20:7 KJV

......

Obscene stories, foolish talk, and coarse jokes—these are not for you. Instead, let there be thankfulness to God.

Ephesians 5:4 NLT

......

Do not let any unwholesome talk come out of your mouths, but only what is helpful for building others up according to their needs, that it may benefit those who listen.

Ephesians 4:29 NIV

Watch your tongue and keep your mouth shut, and you will stay out of trouble.

Proverbs 21:23 NLT

• • • • • •

"But I tell you that everyone will have to give account on the day of judgment for every empty word they have spoken."

Matthew 12:36 NIV

• • • • • •

Let the words of my mouth, and the meditation of my heart, be acceptable in thy sight, O LORD, my strength, and my redeemer.

Psalm 19:14 KJV

Memory Plan

· · · · · · · · · · · · · · · · ·

Memorizing scripture is all about words. When you commit Bible verses to memory, you store God's words in your heart. And when His words are in your heart, you have them ready whenever you need them.

Try memorizing the verses in this chapter without saying them out loud. Write them until you can write them from memory.

Challenge a friend to a game. Both of you look at the scripture reference (for example: Matthew 12:36). Then see if both of you can write its verse correctly. Give yourselves one point for every correctly written verse.

CHAPTER 23

. . . .

GOSSIP

▶▶He Said, She Said

I know a secret. I'll tell you, but don't tell anybody else! Has anyone ever said that to you? Telling secrets about other people is known as "gossip." Gossip is another way of using words in a manner that displeases God.

People who gossip spread rumors. A rumor is something that may or may not be true. When a person spreads a rumor about someone, it can lead to hurt feelings, especially if the rumor is about someone's personal business.

Imagine this. A kid at school doesn't like you, so he spreads a rumor that you got a terrible grade on an easy math test. But you didn't get a terrible grade! In fact, you got all the problems correct. Now, because of that kid's gossip, most of the kids in school think you flunked an easy test. How would that make you feel?

Before speaking about someone, you should always check your words and ask, *Would that please God?*

Gossipers are like Pinocchio. Usually their stories are not the whole truth. So when your ears hear gossip, don't believe everything you hear. Let the gossip end with you. Do that and you will please God.

Memory Verses

. . . .

The book of Proverbs, in the Bible, is filled with good advice.
Here is some of what it says about gossip.

A gossip goes around telling secrets, but those who are
trustworthy can keep a confidence.

Proverbs 11:13 NLT

. . . . . .

A troublemaker plants seeds of strife; gossip separates the best
of friends.

Proverbs 16:28 NLT

. . . . . .

A gossip betrays a confidence; so avoid anyone who talks too
much.

Proverbs 20:19 NIV

Without wood a fire goes out; without a gossip a quarrel dies down.

Proverbs 26:20 NIV

• • • • • •

The words of a gossip are like choice morsels; they go down to the inmost parts.

Proverbs 18:8 NIV

• • • • • •

A gossip goes around telling secrets, so don't hang around with chatterers.

Proverbs 20:19 NLT

Memory Plan

. . . .

Sometimes memorizing scripture is easier if you memorize just one verse a day. Try it and see how it works. Then get your friends together and play this game.

Sit in a circle. You can begin by whispering one of the memory verses to a friend sitting next to you. That person whispers to the next person what he or she heard. See if the verse can get all the way around the circle with all the correct words. Most of the time, it won't.

Remember: That's how gossip goes. As more people repeat it, the truth gets lost.

CHAPTER 24

• • • • • • • • • • • • • •

LYING

▶▶ Pants on Fire!

Liar, liar, pants on fire! Your nose is as long as a telephone wire!
That silly verse has been around a long time. No one knows for
sure where it came from, but kids have said it to call someone
out when they tell a lie.

The rhyme might be funny, but there is nothing funny
about lying. The Bible reminds us, "Lying lips are abomination
to the LORD: but they that deal truly are his delight" (Proverbs
12:22 KJV). *Abomination* is a word that means "disgusting." An
abomination is anything that is unacceptable to God.

Some people think there is nothing wrong with telling a
little-bitty lie. But in God's eyes, there is no difference between
a little lie and a big lie. He always wants the truth.

God is absolutely perfect, and that means He cannot lie.
You can be 100 percent sure that God tells the truth about
everything—always. And that is what He wants you to do, too.
So if ever lying words are about to leave your lips, stop. Tell the
truth. You don't want to get caught with your pants on fire or
your nose as long as a telephone wire!

Memory Verses

Memorize these verses to remind you not to tell lies.

Lying lips are abomination to the LORD: but they that deal truly are his delight.

Proverbs 12:22 KJV

· · · · · ·

God is not a man, so he does not lie. He is not human, so he does not change his mind. Has he ever spoken and failed to act? Has he ever promised and not carried it through?

Numbers 23:19 NLT

· · · · · ·

Thou shalt not bear false witness against thy neighbour.

Exodus 20:16 KJV

Do not lie to each other, since you have taken off your old self with its practices.

Colossians 3:9 NIV

• • • • • •

Rescue me, O LORD, from liars and from all deceitful people.

Psalm 120:2 NLT

• • • • • •

[Satan] has always hated the truth, because there is no truth in him. When he lies, it is consistent with his character; for he is a liar and the father of lies.

John 8:44 NLT

Memory Plan

• • • • • • • • • • • • • • • • •

Try memorizing scripture one word at a time. You will need a partner for this activity and a chalkboard and chalk or a whiteboard and dry-erase marker. Have your partner write a verse on the board and leave out one word. Can you fill in the blank with the correct word? Keep going with your partner removing another word, and then another, until you can fill in all the blanks from memory.

Think about It

· · · · · · · · · · · · · · · · · · · ·

Name three ways that lies can hurt others.

Are small lies okay? Why or why not?

How does lying make you feel?

If you do tell a lie, what should you do?

What is the most important thing you learned while memorizing the verses in this chapter?

God, your heavenly Father, does not lie, but who is the father of lies?

CHAPTER 25

• • • • • • • • • • • • • • •

PRIDE

▶▶ All That and More

She thinks she's all that!

What kind of person do those words describe? Did you say, "Someone full of pride"? *Pride* is a word that means "self-important." Often it is used to describe someone who thinks that she or he is better than everybody else.

The Bible tells about King Nimrod. He wanted the whole world to know that he was all that. So he told his subjects to build a tower all the way to heaven. Nimrod's people were awesome builders. Day after day, their tower got taller. And taller. And taller. Until God stopped them. He knew that King Nimrod was not all that! And God was about to show the whole world that the king was only an ordinary man full of pride.

God messed up everyone's language. None of the builders could understand each other, so they stopped building. In fact, they left Nimrod's kingdom and moved away. They scattered all over the earth.

God hates pride. It's okay to feel good about yourself and what you accomplish. But when you think that you're better than anyone else, God has a problem with that. He likes the opposite of pride—the word for that is *humility*.

Memory Verses

• •

The Bible says this about being all that!

Pride goeth before destruction, and an haughty spirit before a fall.

Proverbs 16:18 KJV

• • • • • •

Pride brings a person low, but the lowly in spirit gain honor.

Proverbs 29:23 NIV

• • • • • •

Though the LORD is great, he cares for the humble, but he keeps his distance from the proud.

Psalm 138:6 NLT

If anyone thinks they are something when they are not, they deceive themselves.

Galatians 6:3 NIV

• • • • • •

This is what the LORD says: "Let not the wise boast of their wisdom or the strong boast of their strength or the rich boast of their riches."

Jeremiah 9:23 NIV

• • • • • •

Do you see a person wise in their own eyes? There is more hope for a fool than for them.

Proverbs 26:12 NIV

Memory Plan

. . . .

Here is a fun way to memorize verses during a quiet time or a rainy day.

You will need a piece of white poster board cut into a 12-inch square. Print one of the verses on the board. Be creative. Fill up the board with your artwork. Now, cut the board into puzzle pieces. Putting the pieces together will help you memorize the verse! Make a bunch of puzzles. Challenge a friend to see who can put a puzzle together the fastest.

CHAPTER 26

. . . .

HUMILITY

▶▶ Humble Like Jesus

Jesus is the perfect example of humility.

Think about who Jesus is. He is the Son of God. He was with God always. He was there with God when God made the earth and everything in it. Jesus is and always will be a part of God.

God sent Jesus to earth on a special mission—to save people from sin and give them life forever in heaven. When Jesus came here, He could have demanded that everyone bow down and worship Him. But He didn't. Instead, Jesus served people by helping them with whatever they needed. Jesus could have used His greatness to save Himself from that awful death on the cross. But He didn't. He put aside His greatness and did what His Father wanted Him to do: complete His mission to save us from sin.

Humility means that you are not selfish. You don't brag about yourself. You are concerned about what happens in the lives of others, and you are willing to help. Sometimes being humble means setting aside something you really want in order to serve someone else. Jesus did all those things, and God wants you to follow His example.

Memory Verses

. . . .

Learn these Bible verses, and remember
that Jesus is the perfect example of humility.

Do nothing out of selfish ambition or vain conceit. Rather, in
humility value others above yourselves, not looking to your
own interests but each of you to the interests of the others.

Philippians 2:3–4 NIV

. . . . . .

In the same way, you who are younger must accept the
authority of the elders. And all of you, dress yourselves in
humility as you relate to one another, for "God opposes the
proud but gives grace to the humble."

1 Peter 5:5 NLT

. . . . . .

So humble yourselves under the mighty power of God, and at
the right time he will lift you up in honor.

1 Peter 5:6 NLT

He guides the humble in what is right and teaches them his way.

Psalm 25:9 NIV

• • • • • •

"God blesses those who are humble, for they will inherit the whole earth."

Matthew 5:5 NLT

• • • • • •

Finally, all of you should be of one mind. Sympathize with each other. Love each other as brothers and sisters. Be tenderhearted, and keep a humble attitude.

1 Peter 3:8 NLT

Memory Plan

• • • • • • • • • • • • • • • • • •

Use one of the tips you have learned so far to memorize the Bible promises in this chapter. Are you pleased that you have memorized so many verses? You should be. Now do something else. Help someone who has trouble memorizing scripture. Do it with humility. You might say things like, "It's okay. It took me awhile to memorize that verse, too." Or you could point out something that the person does well and remind them that they can also get good at memorizing scripture. It's a bonus if you put aside something you wanted to do in order to help someone else.

Think about It

• • • • • • • • • • • • • • • • • • • •

What is pride?

What is humility?

Is it ever okay to be proud of your accomplishments?

If you receive a compliment or an award, how might you show some humility when accepting it?

Why is Jesus a good example of humility?

If you could choose just one memory verse in this chapter to remind you to be humble, which one would you choose?

Midpoint Checkup

You have been working hard to memorize God's words and promises. How have you done so far?

Have you memorized all of the verses in each chapter? If you have, good for you! If not, that's okay, too. It is important to work at a pace that's comfortable for you.

Has it been easy to memorize the verses, or have you found it difficult? If memorizing is hard for you, try not to get discouraged. Reading God's Word is very important, even if you have trouble committing it to memory.

Have you tried some of the Memory Plan ideas? Which did you like best?

Name three things you have learned so far while memorizing the verses in these chapters.

Have you used any of your memorized verses to help you face a challenge or a difficult time?

CHAPTER 27

· · · · · · · · · · · · · · · ·

GUIDANCE

▶▶ Follow the Leader

Imagine that your friend's family has invited you to go on a wilderness camping trip. What fun! But when you get there, you discover something—you are in the middle of nowhere, and nobody in your friend's family has been there before. Everything around you is a mystery.

What do you need? A guide!

A guide is someone who shows you the way. Jesus is the best Guide because one of His purposes here on earth was, and is, to show us the right way to live—the right way is God's way.

Jesus said, "I am the way and the truth and the life. No one comes to the Father except through me" (John 14:6 NIV). That means Jesus shows us the way to God. Jesus is our Guide.

Whenever you feel lost, or when life seems like one big mystery, you can trust Jesus to help you. He always knows God's way, and Jesus never, ever gets lost. So follow Him. Trust Jesus to guide you through your life today and every day.

Memory Verses

Wherever you go, whether with others or alone, you will never be lost, because Jesus is your Guide. This is what the Bible says:

Jesus saith unto him, I am the way, the truth, and the life: no man cometh unto the Father, but by me.

John 14:6 KJV

Whether you turn to the right or to the left, your ears will hear a voice behind you, saying, "This is the way; walk in it."

Isaiah 30:21 NIV

For that is what God is like. He is our God forever and ever, and he will guide us until we die.

Psalm 48:14 NLT

The LORD makes firm the steps of the one who delights in him.

Psalm 37:23 NIV

• • • • • •

Let the morning bring me word of your unfailing love, for I have put my trust in you. Show me the way I should go, for to you I entrust my life.

Psalm 143:8 NIV

• • • • • •

My sheep hear my voice, and I know them, and they follow me.

John 10:27 KJV

Memory Plan

· · · · · · · · · · · · · · · · · ·

It is important to know the scripture reference for every verse you memorize. For example, "My sheep hear my voice, and I know them, and they follow me" is a Bible verse. Its scripture reference is John 10:27 (KJV). The scripture reference tells where to find the verse in the Bible.

Play this Follow the Leader game with your friends. The leader begins walking and calling out Bible memory verses along with their references. If the followers are sure that the verses and references are correct, they follow the leader. But if the leader calls out an incorrect verse and reference, the followers scatter in different directions. See who can lead the group the longest.

CHAPTER 28

· · · · · · · · · · · · · · ·

OBEDIENCE

▶▶ Swallowed Up

Imagine that you are still on that wilderness camping trip. Your guide leads you into the woods. He tells you to listen closely to his words and follow him. But you decide not to obey. Instead, you leave your group and go off on your own. Guess what. You get lost.

Obedience is important, especially when it comes to obeying God. Jonah, in the Bible, found that out the hard way.

God told Jonah to go to a wicked city, Nineveh, and tell the people there to repent—to turn from sin and follow God. But Jonah disobeyed. Instead, he ran away and boarded a ship. While at sea, the ship sailed into a great storm. Jonah told the crew it was his fault the storm had come upon them and told them to throw him overboard. You probably know the rest of the story. A big fish swallowed Jonah, and Jonah sat in its belly for three days before the fish coughed him up. After that, Jonah obeyed God. . . . Wouldn't you?

If you disobey God, you won't end up inside a big fish. But you *will* lose your way. God always knows best. Obey Him.

Memory Verses

· ·

Memorize these verses, and remember to obey God.
Otherwise, you could find yourself swallowed
up by a big mess you've made.

"Now if you will obey me and keep my covenant, you will be
my own special treasure from among all the peoples on earth;
for all the earth belongs to me."

Exodus 19:5 NLT

· · · · · ·

"But I gave them this command: Obey me, and I will be your
God and you will be my people. Walk in obedience to all I
command you, that it may go well with you."

Jeremiah 7:23 NIV

· · · · · ·

But don't just listen to God's word. You must do what it says.
Otherwise, you are only fooling yourselves.

James 1:22 NLT

For if you listen to the word and don't obey, it is like glancing at your face in a mirror. You see yourself, walk away, and forget what you look like.

James 1:23–24 NLT

• • • • • •

And we can be sure that we know him if we obey his commandments.

1 John 2:3 NLT

• • • • • •

But those who obey God's word truly show how completely they love him. That is how we know we are living in him.

1 John 2:5 NLT

Memory Plan

• • • • • • • • • • • • • • • • • •

It is impossible to obey God if you don't know what He expects from you. God's Ten Commandments are a good place to start. After you have memorized the verses in this chapter, read Exodus 20:2–17 in your Bible. Then make a poster of the Ten Commandments and put it in your room where you will see it every day.

1. You shall have no other gods before Me.
2. You shall not make idols.
3. You shall not take the name of the Lord your God in vain.
4. Remember the Sabbath day, to keep it holy.
5. Honor your father and your mother.
6. You shall not murder.
7. You shall not commit adultery.
8. You shall not steal.
9. You shall not bear false witness against your neighbor.
10. You shall not covet.

Talk with your parents or another trusted adult about what each commandment means. Then do your best to obey God's commands.

CHAPTER 29

. . . .

THE BIBLE

▶▶ God's Word

When you walk into a dark room, you turn on a lamp to provide light so you can see where you are going. People need light.

Long ago, in Bible times, a psalmist—a person who writes religious verses to either sing or recite—wrote this: "Thy word is a lamp unto my feet, and a light unto my path" (Psalm 119:105 KJV). He wrote that verse to God, telling Him that His Word—the Bible—is like a bright light that helps people see clearly.

The Bible was written over many years by many different men. All of them knew God and heard His voice, either for real or in their hearts. God told them what to write. The Bible is God's instruction book to all the people on earth. Every word in it is true. That is why reading and memorizing scripture is so important. Scripture is God speaking directly to you through His Bible.

When pastors and others quote the Bible, they sometimes say, "The Bible says." But they could also say, "God says," because every word in the Bible is God's Word.

Think about it. God loves you so much that He wrote a book just for you!

Memory Verses

· · · · · · · · · · · · · · · · · · · ·

Read your Bible every day, because often that is how
God speaks to His people. Sometimes the words will
mean something special to you. And when that happens,
it's a message straight to you from God.
The Bible says this about itself:

And he that sat upon the throne said, Behold, I make all things
new. And he said unto me, Write: for these words are true and
faithful.

Revelation 21:5 KJV

· · · · · ·

All Scripture is inspired by God and is useful to teach us what
is true and to make us realize what is wrong in our lives. It
corrects us when we are wrong and teaches us to do what is
right.

2 Timothy 3:16 NLT

· · · · · ·

In the beginning was the Word, and the Word was with God,
and the Word was God.

John 1:1 KJV

The grass withereth, the flower fadeth: but the word of our God shall stand for ever.

Isaiah 40:8 KJV

• • • • • •

Such things were written in the Scriptures long ago to teach us. And the Scriptures give us hope and encouragement as we wait patiently for God's promises to be fulfilled.

Romans 15:4 NLT

• • • • • •

Heaven and earth shall pass away, but my words shall not pass away.

Matthew 24:35 KJV

Memory Plan

• • • • • • • • • • • • • • • • • •

Most of the books in the Bible were written in Hebrew or
Greek. If you saw the Bible written in those languages, you
probably could not read it.

Here is a fun way to practice memorizing scripture with a
friend. Make up a code for every letter in the alphabet. Then
write a scripture verse from this chapter from memory in code.
Give the coded message to your friend, and see if they can
figure it out. If you can't think of your own code, use this one:

A B C D E F G H I J K L M N O P Q R S T U V W X Y Z
Z Y X W V U T S R Q P O N M L K J I H G F E D C B A

Think about It

• •

The "Word of God" is another name for what?

Is everything in the Bible true? Why or why not?

Why is it important to know what is in the Bible?

When you memorize Bible verses, you are memorizing God's words. Why is that important?

What did you learn about the Bible from this chapter's memory verses?

Name your favorite Bible verse. Why is that one your favorite?

CHAPTER 30

· · · · · · · · · · · · · ·

WISDOM

▶▶ Are You Smart, or Are You Wise?

There is a difference between being smart and being wise. Think of it like this: Imagine reading an entire *Kids' Encyclopedia of Electricity*. You will learn a lot. But will you learn enough to rewire the electricity in your house or fix a power outage in your neighborhood? No. The difference between being smart and being wise is knowing how to put to use what you have learned, or knowing that you are not smart enough to apply what you have learned.

Those guys who tried to build a tower to heaven were smart builders. But they were not wise enough to know what God expected from them. The Bible holds stories of kings and others who were smart but not wise. The ways they used their intelligence were not pleasing to God.

Wisdom comes with knowing God. You learn about Him from reading the Bible, praying, and listening to His voice in your heart. You also learn by observing Him at work in your life and also in the lives of others.

Smart is a good thing to be, but wise is even better. Think of wise ways to use your smartness to please God.

Memory Verses

· · · · · · · · · · · · · · · · · · · ·

Remember, no matter how smart or wise a person is, no one is smarter or wiser than God. Commit these verses to memory.

If you need wisdom [if you want to know what God wants you to do], ask our generous God, and he will give it to you. He will not rebuke you for asking.

James 1:5 NLT

· · · · · ·

I instruct you in the way of wisdom and lead you along straight paths. When you walk, your steps will not be hampered; when you run, you will not stumble.

Proverbs 4:11–12 NIV

· · · · · ·

The foolishness of God is wiser than men; and the weakness of God is stronger than men.

1 Corinthians 1:25 KJV

But the wisdom that comes from heaven is first of all pure; then peace-loving, considerate, submissive, full of mercy and good fruit, impartial and sincere.

James 3:17 NIV

. . . . . .

Don't be impressed with your own wisdom. Instead, fear the LORD and turn away from evil.

Proverbs 3:7 NLT

. . . . . .

Happy is the man that findeth wisdom, and the man that getteth understanding.

Proverbs 3:13 KJV

Memory Plan

Reading and memorizing scripture will make you wise—but only if you meditate on God's words. *Meditate* means "to think deeply" about something. When you meditate on scripture, you think hard about what it means and how it applies to your life.

When you memorize the verses in this chapter, meditate on each one. Pray, and ask God to give you wisdom to know His will for you. Then ask Him to show you how you can use your God-given wisdom to help others.

CHAPTER 31

• • • • • • • • • • • • • •

FRUITFULNESS

▶▶Fruits of the Spirit

So what happens with all that wisdom? It turns into fruit! Not the kind of fruits you eat, but fruits of the Spirit. As God gives you wisdom to know Him, it's like He is watering a young tree—you—to make it grow big and strong. And as you grow in wisdom about God, you begin to produce good "fruit." The Bible says the fruits of the Spirit are love, joy, peace, patience, kindness, goodness, faithfulness, gentleness, and self-control. The Holy Spirit, who is another part of God, like Jesus is, helps the fruits of the Spirit to grow in your heart.

The neat thing about the fruits of the Spirit is that they never run out. There is always plenty of fruit to share with others. And as you share the fruits, more fruit grows! When you share love, joy, peace, patience, kindness, goodness, faithfulness, gentleness, and self-control, you set a good example for others. And if they follow your example, then God's good fruit grows in their hearts, too.

Imagine how loving and peaceful the world would be if everyone became wise and filled up their hearts with God's good fruit.

Memory Verses

. . . .

Memorize these fruitful verses,
and then share a little fruit wherever you go.

But the Holy Spirit produces this kind of fruit in our lives: love, joy, peace, patience, kindness, goodness, faithfulness, gentleness, and self-control. There is no law against these things!

Galatians 5:22–23 NLT

. . . . . .

"This is to my Father's glory, that you bear much fruit, showing yourselves to be my disciples."

John 15:8 NIV

. . . . . .

"No good tree bears bad fruit, nor does a bad tree bear good fruit."

Luke 6:43 NIV

"Each tree is recognized by its own fruit. People do not pick figs from thornbushes, or grapes from briers."

Luke 6:44 NIV

• • • • • •

Wherefore by their fruits ye shall know them.

Matthew 7:20 KJV

• • • • • •

But they delight in the law of the LORD, meditating on it day and night. They are like trees planted along the riverbank, bearing fruit each season. Their leaves never wither, and they prosper in all they do.

Psalm 1:2–3 NLT

Memory Plan

. . . .

Memorizing verses about good fruit will help you to recognize it in others. You will notice that some people do not produce good fruit. Instead, their fruit is like rotten apples and sour, spoiled grapes. Bad fruit often turns into evil, and there is enough of that in the world.

Learn to recognize good fruit when you see it. Make a scrapbook of this chapter's memory verses. Add drawings and newspaper articles that show good fruit in action. Finally, come up with some ideas of your own to share good fruit in your neighborhood and community.

CHAPTER 32

· · · · · · · · · · · · · · ·

TEMPTATION

▶▶ Willpower!

Oh, those brownies look so good! Fudgy. Chewy. Chocolate. But your mom said you can't have even one. Those brownies are not for you. They are for her book club. But you want one. So bad. Will she notice if just one is missing?

Willpower, or self-control, is hard, especially when you really, really want something and can't have it. Satan—the devil—loves tempting your willpower. He will try every day. He even tried tempting Jesus.

Satan took Jesus up a very high mountain, to its very peak. From there, he showed Jesus all the kingdoms in the world, kingdoms rich in every way, dripping with gold and silver and filled with wonderful things. And Satan said to Jesus, "I will give it all to You if You will kneel down and worship me."

But Jesus stood up to Satan with mighty strength and will-power. "Get out of here, Satan," He said. "For the Scriptures say, 'You must worship the LORD your God and serve only him'" (Matthew 4:10 NLT).

Satan obeyed and went away.

Whenever you are tempted by something you shouldn't have, be like Jesus. Stand strong. Show your willpower, and chase the devil away.

Memory Verses

. . . .

These verses are like armor against Satan's temptations.
Learn them and use them whenever you feel tempted.

"Get out of here, Satan," Jesus told him. "For the Scriptures say,
'You must worship the LORD your God and serve only him.'"

Matthew 4:10 NLT

. . . . . .

And lead us not into temptation, but deliver us from evil:
For thine is the kingdom, and the power, and the glory, for ever.
Amen.

Matthew 6:13 KJV

. . . . . .

The temptations in your life are no different from what
others experience. And God is faithful. He will not allow the
temptation to be more than you can stand. When you are
tempted, he will show you a way out so that you can endure.

1 Corinthians 10:13 NLT

"Watch and pray so that you will not fall into temptation. The spirit is willing, but the flesh is weak."

Matthew 26:41 NIV

• • • • • •

Submit yourselves therefore to God. Resist the devil, and he will flee from you.

James 4:7 KJV

• • • • • •

God blesses those who patiently endure testing and temptation. Afterward they will receive the crown of life that God has promised to those who love him.

James 1:12 NLT

Memory Plan

· · · · · · · · · · · · · · · · · · ·

Temptation often comes disguised as peer pressure or in innocent little tempts, like a plate of forbidden brownies. Learn to recognize temptation when you see it. This week, test your willpower. Make a list of all the ways Satan tries to tempt you, and write down the memory verse you use to chase him away. At the end of the week, count all the items on your list. You will see that Satan is always busy trying to get you to turn away from God. Did you give in to his temptation? If so, ask God to forgive you. He will. God knows that no one is perfect.

Think about It

· · · · · · · · · · · · · · · · · · ·

How would you explain "temptation" to a younger brother or sister?

If you felt tempted to do something that you know is wrong, what would you do?

Name a time when you were tempted and gave in to temptation.

Name a time when you were tempted but didn't give in.

Did you feel tempted not to memorize all the verses in this chapter? Who do you think put that idea in your head?

Which of the memory verses in this chapter is your favorite?

CHAPTER 33

· · · · · · · · · · · · ·

MONEY

▶▶I Want That!

Is there something you want, but it is too expensive? When you see something you like in an advertisement, do you say, "I want that"? We live in a world where money buys things. And if you have enough money, you can buy just about anything you want.

Money is a good thing when it buys what we need. But money is not so good when we need more and more of it to get what we want.

Jesus told a rich man to give up everything he owned and follow Him. The man had lots of money. He had everything he wanted. The idea of giving it all up to follow Jesus was just too much. So the man walked away.

Jesus knew the man's heart. He knew that the things he owned were so important to the man that he wouldn't give them up. Not even to God. That is when money becomes trouble, when it becomes way too important in someone's life.

Money comes with responsibility. God expects you to use your money wisely, not selfishly. So always put God first. Pray. Ask Him to show you what to do with your money. And think before you spend.

Memory Verses

. . . .

This is what the Bible says about money:

Jesus answered, "If you want to be perfect, go, sell your possessions and give to the poor, and you will have treasure in heaven. Then come, follow me."

Matthew 19:21 NIV

. . . . . .

"No one can serve two masters. Either you will hate the one and love the other, or you will be devoted to the one and despise the other. You cannot serve both God and money."

Matthew 6:24 NIV

. . . . . .

Keep your lives free from the love of money and be content with what you have, because God has said, "Never will I leave you; never will I forsake you."

Hebrews 13:5 NIV

For the love of money is the root of all kinds of evil. And some people, craving money, have wandered from the true faith and pierced themselves with many sorrows.

1 Timothy 6:10 NLT

• • • • • •

For where your treasure is, there will your heart be also.

Matthew 6:21 KJV

• • • • • •

Honor the LORD with your wealth and with the best part of everything you produce.

Proverbs 3:9 NLT

Memory Plan

. . . .

What if Jesus said to you, "Give up everything you want to do, and spend the whole afternoon memorizing scripture"? Would you do it? Would you do it willingly? It's hard giving up what you want, even when it means pleasing God. Still, whenever you put God first, you honor Him, respect Him, and show Him that you love Him.

Spend extra time today memorizing the verses in this chapter. Give up something that you want to do to spend more time with God.

CHAPTER 34

. . . .

ETERNAL LIFE

▶▶ The Needle's Eye

A rich man rode his camel through the desert. The man gave the camel commands, and the camel obeyed. This pleased the man, because he was used to getting everything he wanted. Gold. Silver. Jewels. He had enough money to buy them all.

After a while, they came to a needle sticking up from the sand. Because the man was used to getting whatever he wanted, he demanded that the camel walk through the eye of the needle. Could the camel do it?

Of course not! All the money in the world can't put a camel through a needle's eye.

Jesus used this example when speaking to His disciples. He said, "It is easier for a camel to go through the eye of a needle than for someone who is rich to enter the kingdom of God." He meant that all the money in the world cannot buy forever life in heaven.

Forever life, or *eternal* life, is God's gift to anyone who believes that Jesus died for their sins. It is why God sent Jesus to die on the cross. His precious gift is your ticket to living with God forever in heaven. And that is something money can't buy.

Memory Verses

Eternal life means that when you die, your soul, the part that makes you *you*, goes to heaven to live there with God forever. Memorize these verses about eternal life.

And this is what he promised us—eternal life.

1 John 2:25 NIV

• • • • • •

Jesus said unto her, I am the resurrection, and the life: he that believeth in me, though he were dead, yet shall he live.

John 11:25 KJV

• • • • • •

And whosoever liveth and believeth in me shall never die. Believest thou this?

John 11:26 KJV

"There is more than enough room in my Father's home. If this were not so, would I have told you that I am going to prepare a place for you? When everything is ready, I will come and get you, so that you will always be with me where I am."

John 14:2–3 NLT

· · · · · ·

Now this is eternal life: that they know you, the only true God, and Jesus Christ, whom you have sent.

John 17:3 NIV

· · · · · ·

For since we believe that Jesus died and was raised to life again, we also believe that when Jesus returns, God will bring back with him the believers who have died.

1 Thessalonians 4:14 NLT

Memory Plan

• • • • • • • • • • • • • • • • •

If someone you know should die, the verses in this chapter will help you to feel better. Memorize them and store them in your heart. Remember that although you can't see Christians who have died, they are still happy and alive in heaven. And if you believe in Jesus' gift of eternal life, you will see those people again when you get to heaven someday.

Draw a picture of what you think heaven looks like. Write out one of the memory verses from this chapter on your picture.

CHAPTER 35

• • • • • • • • • • • • • •

THE HOLY SPIRIT

▶▶ The Comforter

Everyone feels uncomfortable sometimes. An unfamiliar situation, like the first day of school, can make you feel uncomfortable. Your body can feel uncomfortable, too, when you are sick or hurting. And feelings, like sadness, can be uncomfortable.

God understands. He wants people to feel good and loved. So God gives us a special part of Himself—a part called the Comforter.

The Comforter part of God has another name: the Holy Spirit. The Holy Spirit is also called the Helper. In an uncomfortable situation, the Comforter gives you courage. When your body is sick, the Comforter provides the help that you need to be well again. And when you feel sad, the Comforter helps you remember that things will get better. Like Jesus, the Holy Spirit is an invisible friend. And unlike an imaginary friend who is not real, the Holy Spirit *is* real, just like God the Father and Jesus the Son are real. The Holy Spirit is with you all the time and forever.

The Holy Spirit does other things, too. He helps you to pray and make good decisions. And He teaches you right from wrong. The Holy Spirit lives inside your heart with God and Jesus.

Memory Verses

• • • • • • • • • • • • • • • • • • • •

Isn't the heavenly Father amazing? He doesn't give us only
a part of Himself, but all of Himself—God as Father;
Jesus, His Son; and the Holy Spirit, the Comforter!
The Bible tells us more about the Holy Spirit:

And I will pray the Father, and he shall give you another
Comforter, that he may abide with you for ever.

John 14:16 KJV

• • • • • •

I will not leave you comfortless: I will come to you.

John 14:18 KJV

• • • • • •

"But the Advocate, the Holy Spirit, whom the Father will send
in my name, will teach you all things and will remind you of
everything I have said to you."

John 14:26 NIV

And the Holy Spirit helps us in our weakness. For example, we don't know what God wants us to pray for. But the Holy Spirit prays for us with groanings that cannot be expressed in words.

Romans 8:26 NLT

• • • • • •

For we know how dearly God loves us, because he has given us the Holy Spirit to fill our hearts with his love.

Romans 5:5 NLT

• • • • • •

So I say, let the Holy Spirit guide your lives. Then you won't be doing what your sinful nature craves.

Galatians 5:16 NLT

Memory Plan

• • • • • • • • • • • • • • • • • •

Here is a fun way for you and a friend to memorize scripture.
Break up a Bible verse into words or short parts, and write
each word or part on an index card or a small piece of paper.
Then have one person hide all the parts. That person gives clues
about where to find each part, in order. The other player must
find and memorize each part before moving on. When all of
the parts have been found, the player must recite the whole
verse from memory.

Think about It

• • • • • • • • • • • • • • • • • • •

Name a time when you felt uncomfortable. What made you feel better?

God divides Himself into three special parts. The first two are the heavenly Father and His Son, Jesus. What is the name of the third part of God?

Name three things the Holy Spirit does.

The Holy Spirit is sometimes called the Comforter and what else?

Do you think the Holy Spirit could help you to memorize a long Bible verse? Why or why not?

How can the memory verses in this chapter help when you feel uncomfortable?

CHAPTER 36

• • • • • • • • • • • • • •

JOY!

▶▶ Rejoice!

Maybe you have heard the phrase "filled with the Holy Spirit." The Holy Spirit can fill people up with joy.

There is great joy just knowing that God is GOD. The fact that He made you should bring you much joy. After all, without Him, wonderful you wouldn't be here! And God loves you so much that He makes His home inside your heart. That's another good reason to be joyful. And God thinks that you are so special that He hangs out with you all the time. That's a great reason to be joyful. If you think about it, you will find all sorts of reasons to find joy in the Lord.

In his letter to the Philippians, the apostle Paul wrote, "Rejoice in the Lord always. I will say it again: Rejoice!" (Philippians 4:4 NIV). *Rejoice* is a word that means "to feel or show great joy."

Sometimes, everyday life gets in the way of joyfulness, and then you think about what is wrong instead of what is right. The Holy Spirit can help with that. When things go wrong, ask Him to remind you of good things in your life. Then follow Paul's instructions and do it—REJOICE!

Memory Verses

Think about and memorize these joyful Bible verses.

Rejoice in the Lord always: and again I say, Rejoice.

Philippians 4:4 KJV

• • • • • •

This is the day which the LORD hath made; we will rejoice and be glad in it.

Psalm 118:24 KJV

• • • • • •

The LORD is my strength and my shield; my heart trusts in him, and he helps me. My heart leaps for joy, and with my song I praise him.

Psalm 28:7 NIV

Let the whole world sing for joy, because you govern the nations with justice and guide the people of the whole world.

Psalm 67:4 NLT

• • • • • •

Be joyful in hope, patient in affliction, faithful in prayer.

Romans 12:12 NIV

• • • • • •

You who are young, be happy while you are young, and let your heart give you joy in the days of your youth. Follow the ways of your heart and whatever your eyes see, but know that for all these things God will bring you into judgment.

Ecclesiastes 11:9 NIV

Memory Plan

● ● ● ● ● ● ● ● ● ● ● ● ● ● ● ● ●

Memorize the verses in this chapter with your friends. Talk about what each verse means. Then make up some cheers about joy! Have fun adding actions and dance moves to your cheers.

Here is a cheer based on Psalm 67:4 to get you started:

> *Hey there, World. Shout for joy.*
> *J–O–Y!*
> *Because God rules. Yes, He rules!*
> *J–O–Y!*
> *He guides His people!*
> *Rules with justice!*
> *J–O–Y!*
> *Hey there, World. Shout for joy!*
> *Yay, God!*

CHAPTER 37

. . . .

HOPE

▶▶ A Hopeful Heart

The New Testament tells about a woman with a blood disease. For twelve years she suffered from her sickness, traveling from doctor to doctor, hoping for a cure. No one could help her. This woman spent her money on doctors until finally she used it all up, her whole life savings! Still, she hung on to hope.

She heard of a man named Jesus, a Teacher and Healer. Maybe He could help. But Jesus traveled with big crowds of people.

I could never get His attention, the woman thought. *But maybe, if I can just touch Him, it will be enough.* She hoped.

She went to where Jesus was and pushed through the big crowd that followed Him. She reached out and barely touched the hem of His robe—and do you know what?

Jesus felt that little, hope-filled touch! He turned to the woman and healed her.

Jesus is your hope, too. Whenever you feel like giving up, keep on hoping in Him. Jesus knows what is going on with you right now. He knows what you hope for and also what you need. So whenever you want His attention, just ask. He is right there waiting inside your heart.

Memory Verses

· ·

Memorize these hopeful verses.

And so, Lord, where do I put my hope? My only hope is in you.

Psalm 39:7 NLT

· · · · · ·

You will be secure, because there is hope; you will look about you and take your rest in safety.

Job 11:18 NIV

· · · · · ·

Guide me in your truth and teach me, for you are God my Savior, and my hope is in you all day long.

Psalm 25:5 NIV

Why am I discouraged? Why is my heart so sad? I will put my hope in God! I will praise him again.

Psalm 42:5 NLT

• • • • • •

The Lord is good unto them that wait for him, to the soul that seeketh him.

Lamentations 3:25 KJV

• • • • • •

But as for me, I watch in hope for the Lord, I wait for God my Savior; my God will hear me.

Micah 7:7 NIV

Memory Plan

· · · · · · · · · · · · · · · · · · ·

After you have memorized the verses in this chapter, ask your pastor if you can make some hope cards for him or her to take along on visits to shut-ins from your church. A hope card is a card that you make and decorate with one of the hope verses written inside. Elderly people and the sick love getting hopeful cards, and you can spread hope around by making some for your church family. Can you think of others outside of your church who might need a hope card?

CHAPTER 38

. . . .

PERSEVERANCE

▶▶ The Finish Line

Have you ever stood at the finish line of a triathlon? Most of the competitors look worn out, don't they? They have been through a lot—swimming, biking, and running for miles. Still, most of them hung in there and finished the race. There is a word for sticking with something to the finish. That word is *perseverance*.

Noah persevered when he built the ark. If he had given up without finishing, none of the world's animals or people would have survived the big flood, and today the earth might be empty of any living thing.

And Paul never gave up, either. He kept on telling people about Jesus until the day he died. He persevered through three shipwrecks, beatings, and people trying to kill him by pelting him with stones.

At times you might feel like giving up when something seems too big or too hard. That's when you need to call on God. If you are working to finish something good, then He will give you everything you need to accomplish your goal.

Keep running toward that finish line. If you need help with perseverance, say a prayer right now and ask God to help you.

Memory Verses

• •

Persevere until you have finished
memorizing all of these verses.

So let's not get tired of doing what is good. At just the right
time we will reap a harvest of blessing if we don't give up.

Galatians 6:9 NLT

• • • • • •

Therefore, my dear brothers and sisters, stand firm. Let nothing
move you. Always give yourselves fully to the work of the Lord,
because you know that your labor in the Lord is not in vain.

1 Corinthians 15:58 NIV

• • • • • •

Don't you realize that in a race everyone runs, but only one
person gets the prize? So run to win!

1 Corinthians 9:24 NLT

Better is the end of a thing than the beginning thereof: and the patient in spirit is better than the proud in spirit.

Ecclesiastes 7:8 KJV

• • • • • •

I have fought a good fight, I have finished my course, I have kept the faith.

2 Timothy 4:7 KJV

• • • • • •

Now you should finish what you started. Let the eagerness you showed in the beginning be matched now by your giving. Give in proportion to what you have.

2 Corinthians 8:11 NLT

Memory Plan

Everyone has times when they say, "I should be doing (this or that)." It's normal to want to put off things that are time-consuming or hard. Memorizing scripture is something you might not always want to do. But it is a necessary thing because knowing God's Word is how you get to know God.

Whenever you feel like putting off memorizing Bible verses, keep your eyes on Jesus, and do it for Him. Jesus never gave up. Even when He was tired, He kept on helping people and doing what is right.

How would you feel if Jesus gave up on you? He won't. Not ever. So honor Him by memorizing God's Word and keeping it in your heart.

Think about It

. . . .

Do you give up easily or do you persevere?

When you feel like giving up, what helps you to keep going?

What advice would you give to a friend who feels like giving up?

Which is your favorite memory verse in this chapter?

Do you have trouble memorizing Bible verses? What might help you to persevere?

Name a time when you wanted to give up but kept going. What did you learn from not giving up?

CHAPTER 39

• • • • • • • • • • • • • •

CHILDREN

▶▶ Kids Are Special

God loves kids. When you read your Bible, you will discover that David was a kid when he stood up to that mean giant, Goliath. The story of Joseph in the Bible begins when he was a kid. So does the story of Moses. He was a baby in a basket when Pharaoh's daughter found him in the bulrushes. And God could have sent Jesus to earth as a man, but instead He sent Him as a baby. Jesus had a childhood, like you do. He played and learned before He became an adult.

Jesus loves kids. When His disciples tried to keep little children from coming to Him, Jesus did not like it. He welcomed children. And who saved the day when there was not enough food for a crowd listening to Jesus preach? A kid with five small loaves of bread and two fish. With Jesus' help, his lunch fed more than five thousand people!

Do you know that God loves you just as much as He loved kids in Bible times? He does! You are super special to Him. God is your heavenly Father. He was with you before you were born, and He will be with you forever. And that's a promise!

Memory Verses

· · · · · · · · · · · · · · · · · · · ·

The Bible includes these verses about kids.
Remember them because they are especially for you.

Children are a gift from the LORD; they are a reward from him.

Psalm 127:3 NLT

· · · · · ·

You must remain faithful to the things you have been taught.
You know they are true, for you know you can trust those who
taught you.

2 Timothy 3:14 NLT

· · · · · ·

You have taught children and infants to tell of your strength.

Psalm 8:2 NLT

And [Jesus] said: "Truly I tell you, unless you change and become like little children, you will never enter the kingdom of heaven.

Matthew 18:3 NIV

• • • • • •

Then he put a little child among them. Taking the child in his arms, he said to them, "Anyone who welcomes a little child like this on my behalf welcomes me, and anyone who welcomes me welcomes not only me but also my Father who sent me."

Mark 9:36–37 NLT

• • • • • •

Train up a child in the way he should go: and when he is old, he will not depart from it.

Proverbs 22:6 KJV

Memory Plan

Do you like to write and draw? You can share your special drawings and words in a journal. Use a blank notebook, and give it the title "God and Me." Then, every day or as often as you like, write or draw your thoughts about God. Begin each entry with a memory verse. Use verses that you have learned in this book and others that you know.

You can use your journal to write letters to God and tell Him your thoughts. You can also use it to write stories and poems about things you learn from the Bible.

CHAPTER 40

· · · · · · · · · · · · ·

WORRY/ANXIETY

▶▶The What-If Worries

Everyone feels nervous sometimes. Feeling nervous is a normal part of life. Kids get nervous feelings. Grown-ups do, too. When you feel worried and nervous, maybe your belly hurts or does flip-flops, or maybe your hands get sweaty and you get really quiet. Each person's body reacts differently to worry.

Nervous feelings usually come from a bad case of the what-ifs. *What if I don't like my new school? What if I forget my lines in the play? What if I don't like riding in an airplane?* If the what-if worries swirl around you like a swarm of hungry mosquitoes, there's something you can do.

Swat them! Yes, swat those worrisome what-if thoughts, and make them leave you alone. You can swat them by turning your thoughts toward God.

Jesus said that God is always in control. He said that if God takes care of little things like flowers and birds, then He most certainly takes care of people. And He most certainly takes care of *you!*

God loves you. He will take care of you wherever you go. So stop those what-ifs as soon as they start. Trust God to help you be calm.

Memory Verses

• • • • • • • • • • • • • • • • • • • •

Whenever you get the what-if worries, remember these verses.
Use them to help stop those sweaty palms and belly flip-flops.

Don't worry about anything; instead, pray about everything.
Tell God what you need, and thank him for all he has done.

Philippians 4:6 NLT

• • • • • •

"Look at the birds of the air; they do not sow or reap or store
away in barns, and yet your heavenly Father feeds them. Are
you not much more valuable than they?"

Matthew 6:26 NIV

• • • • • •

"Can any one of you by worrying add a single hour to your
life?"

Matthew 6:27 NIV

"And if God cares so wonderfully for wildflowers that are here today and thrown into the fire tomorrow, he will certainly care for you. Why do you have so little faith?"

Matthew 6:30 NLT

• • • • • •

Cast all your anxiety on him because he cares for you.

1 Peter 5:7 NIV

• • • • • •

Anxiety weighs down the heart, but a kind word cheers it up.

Proverbs 12:25 NIV

Memory Plan

. . . .

The Bible compares God to a rock. Think about the biggest, hardest rock you have ever seen. A big rock is tough. It can stand up to anything—storms, fires, floods, *anything*. Now remember that God is stronger than a rock.

Whenever you feel nervous, find a small stone and keep it in your pocket. Every time a what-if worry comes your way, touch the stone and recite one of the verses you memorized from this chapter. Then remember that God is with you. He is like a big, strong rock, and He cares for you all the time, wherever you go.

CHAPTER 41

· · · · · · · · · · · · · · ·

PRIORITIES

▶▶ Putting God First

When Jesus traveled, He didn't stay in a hotel like people do today. He relied on the hospitality of others. Often, people welcomed Jesus into their homes for a meal or to spend the night.

Two sisters, Mary and Martha, were Jesus' close friends. One day Jesus and His disciples stopped at their house. The sisters might not have expected them, because Martha got busy in the kitchen making a meal for the group. While Martha cooked, Mary did nothing but sit and listen to Jesus speak. That upset Martha. She said to Jesus, "Lord, doesn't it seem unfair to You that my sister just sits here while I do all the work? Tell her to come and help me."

Jesus' answer might surprise you. He said, "My dear Martha, you are worried and upset over all these details! There is only one thing worth being concerned about. Mary has discovered it, and it will not be taken away from her" (Luke 10:41–42 NLT).

Jesus meant that nothing is more important than listening to Him. He should come before everything else.

Do you always put Jesus first? Is anything in your life more important to you than Him?

Memory Verses

· ·

Prioritize is a word that means "to make one thing more important than another." Use these memory verses to remind you that nothing is more important than God.

Jesus said unto him, Thou shalt love the Lord thy God with all thy heart, and with all thy soul, and with all thy mind.

Matthew 22:37 KJV

· · · · · ·

Thou shalt have no other gods before me.

Exodus 20:3 KJV

· · · · · ·

"Seek the Kingdom of God above all else, and live righteously, and he will give you everything you need."

Matthew 6:33 NLT

"I am the vine; you are the branches. If you remain in me and I in you, you will bear much fruit; apart from me you can do nothing."

John 15:5 NIV

• • • • • •

"He must become greater and greater, and I must become less and less."

John 3:30 NLT

• • • • • •

I am Alpha and Omega, the beginning and the end, the first and the last.

Revelation 22:13 KJV

Memory Plan

• • • • • • • • • • • • • • • • • •

If you believe that God is the one and only God, that means there are no other gods you believe in or worship—you put Him first. When you thank God for your food before you eat a meal, then you make Him more important than eating. When you pray before you go to bed at night, then you make God more important than falling asleep.

As you memorize the verses in this chapter, think about putting God first all the time. Then make a list of all the ways you can think of to put God before the other things in your life. Put into action those things on your list.

Think about It

· · · · · · · · · · · · · · · · · · ·

What have you learned from memorizing the verses in this chapter?

Why is it so important to always put God first?

God said, "Thou shalt have no other gods before me." Can you name some things that might be other gods? Hint: Think about some things that people sometimes make more important than God.

Have some things in your life become more important to you than God? If so, remember that you can ask God to forgive you, and He will.

What can you do to help you remember to always put God first?

Can you share some ideas with your family about making God the priority in your home?

CHAPTER 42

. . . .

STRENGTH

▶▶ Strong in Spirit

What do you think of when you hear the word *strong*? A guy with big, bulging muscles? Someone lifting weights? Or maybe you think of a superhero picking up a cement truck as if it were a toy.

A powerful body is one way to think of strength, but there is another, even better, way to be strong: *strong in spirit.*

Being strong in spirit means that your heart is like steel when anything threatens your faith in God. If someone says, "God is not real," your spirit—where God lives in your heart— shouts, "Yes, He *is* real!" Nothing at all can change your mind, because your trust in God is so strong.

A strong spirit is tough, like steel. Everything bounces off of it. If someone makes fun of you because you are a Christian, their words will bounce off your strong spirit. If something bad happens and Satan says, "See, God doesn't love you," your strong spirit will shout, "Yes, God *does* love me!"

When you put all of your faith and trust in God, He gives your spirit superpower strength so that nothing can get between you and Him.

Memory Verses

· ·

The Bible says this about being strong in spirit:

I pray that from his glorious, unlimited resources he will empower you with inner strength through his Spirit.

Ephesians 3:16 NLT

· · · · · ·

He gives strength to the weary and increases the power of the weak.

Isaiah 40:29 NIV

· · · · · ·

The Sovereign LORD is my strength! He makes me as surefooted as a deer, able to tread upon the heights.

Habakkuk 3:19 NLT

God is our refuge and strength, a very present help in trouble.

Psalm 46:1 KJV

• • • • • •

God is my strength and power: and he maketh my way perfect.

2 Samuel 22:33 KJV

• • • • • •

Finally, be strong in the Lord and in his mighty power.

Ephesians 6:10 NIV

Memory Plan

· · · · · · · · · · · · · · · · · ·

When anything threatens your faith in God, you can use all of the memory verses in this chapter to remind you to be strong.

Make a Strength of Spirit paper chain to help you remember.

1. Measure and cut six strips of paper that are even in length and width. Make them big enough to write one memory verse on each.

2. Write a memory verse on your first strip. Then tape the ends of the first strip together to form a loop.

3. Write a memory verse on the second strip. Place the second strip of paper through the loop of the first strip, and join the ends together with tape.

4. Keep going until you have made a chain of this chapter's six memory verses.

CHAPTER 43

· · · · · · · · · · · · · · ·

LAZINESS

▶▶ Lazybones

Lazybones is a word used to describe a lazy person—one who would rather do nothing than work. Proverbs 6:6–11 (NLT) says:

> Take a lesson from the ants, you lazybones.
>   Learn from their ways and become wise!
> Though they have no prince
>   or governor or ruler to make them work,
> they labor hard all summer,
>   gathering food for the winter.
> But you, lazybones, how long will you sleep?
>   When will you wake up?
> A little extra sleep, a little more slumber,
>   a little folding of the hands to rest—
> then poverty will pounce on you like a bandit;
>   scarcity will attack you like an armed robber."
>
> (Proverbs 6:6–11 NLT)

Ants might be small, but they are never lazy. They build tunnels underground and protect the entrances with hills of sand. They work together finding food and carrying it through the tunnels to store up for winter. Take a good, long look at ants, and you will see that they are always busy.

Are you like an ant, or are you a lazybones?

Memory Verses

. . . .

Don't be a lazybones! Get busy and memorize these verses.

Take a lesson from the ants, you lazybones. Learn from their
ways and become wise!

Proverbs 6:6 NLT

. . . . . .

A little extra sleep, a little more slumber, a little folding of the
hands to rest—then poverty will pounce on you like a bandit;
scarcity will attack you like an armed robber.

Proverbs 6:10–11 NLT

. . . . . .

A sluggard's appetite is never filled, but the desires of the
diligent are fully satisfied.

Proverbs 13:4 NIV

Those who work their land will have abundant food, but those who chase fantasies will have their fill of poverty.

Proverbs 28:19 NIV

• • • • • •

Work hard and become a leader; be lazy and become a slave.

Proverbs 12:24 NLT

• • • • • •

Never be lazy, but work hard and serve the Lord enthusiastically.

Romans 12:11 NLT

Memory Plan

. . . .

The book of Proverbs in the Bible is a book of wisdom. A proverb is a little piece of wise advice. Most of the memory verses in this chapter come from the book of Proverbs, and all of them offer advice that is good and true. When you memorize and put proverbs into action, you live in a way that is pleasing to God.

You have already memorized many Bible promises, and in doing so you have grown in wisdom about living as a Christian.

Try this. Write some of your own proverbs. Create your own little bits of advice based on what you have learned from the verses you have memorized.

CHAPTER 44

· · · · · · · · · · · · · · · ·

MERCY

▶▶ God's Free Pass

When you misbehave, you usually receive some sort of punishment. Maybe your parent sends you to your room or takes away some of your privileges. Wrongdoing has its consequences. But have you ever received a free pass—a time when you deserved to be punished, but your parents decided to talk with you about what you did wrong instead of punishing you? Deserving punishment but receiving a free pass is called *mercy*.

Because God is our heavenly Father, He acts like a parent. He sometimes punishes people for misbehaving, and sometimes He gives them a free pass—He teaches them gently and responds with mercy. Mercy is a special gift from God.

All humans sin. That is because no one except God is perfect. Sin is bad behavior, and bad behavior has consequences. But when God forgives sin without punishment, He shows humans mercy. Jesus was merciful to us by taking on our sins so we can be sinless when we go to heaven.

Can you think of other examples of mercy?

Memory Verses

· ·

Add these Bible verses to the list of those you have memorized.

For thou, Lord, art good, and ready to forgive; and plenteous in mercy unto all them that call upon thee.

Psalm 86:5 KJV

· · · · · ·

"Be merciful, just as your Father is merciful."

Luke 6:36 NIV

· · · · · ·

All praise to God, the Father of our Lord Jesus Christ. It is by his great mercy that we have been born again, because God raised Jesus Christ from the dead. Now we live with great expectation.

1 Peter 1:3 NLT

Let us therefore come boldly unto the throne of grace, that we may obtain mercy, and find grace to help in time of need.

Hebrews 4:16 KJV

• • • • • •

The LORD is good to all: and his tender mercies are over all his works.

Psalm 145:9 KJV

• • • • • •

Surely goodness and mercy shall follow me all the days of my life: and I will dwell in the house of the LORD for ever.

Psalm 23:6 KJV

Memory Plan

· · · · · · · · · · · · · · · · · ·

Maybe you have had trouble memorizing some of these Bible promises. And maybe there are times when you have been—well—a lazybones when it comes to memorizing scripture. Don't worry. God loves you. He understands and will have mercy on you.

Spend some time telling God you haven't always done so well at memorizing Bible verses. Then ask Him for mercy, and ask Him to help you. Maybe there is some special way to make it easier for you to memorize scripture. Ask God to help you find it.

Think about It

. . . .

What is mercy?

Name a time when someone showed you mercy.

Name a time when you were merciful toward someone else.

Why do you think God shows mercy toward His people?

If you were praying to God about His mercy, what would you say?

Why do you think it is important to memorize scripture verses about God's mercy?

CHAPTER 45

• • • • • • • • • • • • •

CHARITY

▶▶ Feel-Good Giving

The Gospels—the Bible books of Matthew, Mark, Luke, and John—are all about Jesus. They include the exact words that He spoke. Maybe your Bible has Jesus' words printed in red so they stand out. Isn't it wonderful knowing what He had to say?

"The Lord Jesus himself said: 'It is more blessed to give than to receive'" (Acts 20:35 NIV). He meant that giving to others fills up your heart with good feelings.

If you rescued an animal from a shelter and gave it a happy home, wouldn't that make you feel good? And when you help your parents without being asked and you get a big hug, that feels good, too, doesn't it?

Charity is a word that means "giving to those in need." Charity is giving your skills, time, or money to help others while expecting nothing in return. You can practice charity by giving food to a food bank and clothing to a thrift shop. Or you could volunteer to help at church, at school, and in your community. Can you think of other ways to practice charity?

Try to be charitable today and every day. The more you give, the more your heart will fill up with good feelings.

Memory Verses

• •

Remember these six verses about charity.
Then think of ways that you can be charitable to others.

"Give, and it will be given to you. A good measure, pressed down,
shaken together and running over, will be poured into your lap.
For with the measure you use, it will be measured to you."

Luke 6:38 NIV

• • • • • •

Oh, the joys of those who are kind to the poor! The Lord
rescues them when they are in trouble.

Psalm 41:1 NLT

• • • • • •

And now abideth faith, hope, charity, these three; but the
greatest of these is charity.

1 Corinthians 13:13 KJV

Each of you should give what you have decided in your heart to give, not reluctantly or under compulsion, for God loves a cheerful giver.

2 Corinthians 9:7 NIV

. . . . . .

Give to him that asketh thee, and from him that would borrow of thee turn not thou away.

Matthew 5:42 KJV

. . . . . .

For I was an hungred, and ye gave me meat: I was thirsty, and ye gave me drink: I was a stranger, and ye took me in.

Matthew 25:35 KJV

Memory Plan

You are doing a great job memorizing scripture! And along the way, you have been learning to make scripture easier to memorize and put into action. Now you can add "memorizing scripture" to your list of skills!

People are often in need of Bible verses that are special to them. Here is one way to share your scripture skills with others. Think of a memory verse that reminds you of a family member or friend. Then make a Thinking about You card that says: *This Bible verse reminds me of you.* Add the verse. Write it from memory. Then give the card to the person. Don't stop with just one card, but make plenty to give away. How about making one for your pastor or Sunday school teacher? How about a grandparent, brother, or sister?

CHAPTER 46

• • • • • • • • • • • • • •

GOD THE FATHER

▶▶ Your Heavenly Father

Families come in all sizes. Some are small, maybe just a mother or dad and a child. Other families are big. And if you count grandparents, aunts, uncles, and cousins, some families are huge!

The biggest family of all is God's family. His family is made up of all the people on earth—not just living now, but all of the people who have ever lived and all those who haven't been born yet.

Because God is the head of all families on earth, He is called our heavenly Father. God is a perfect and magnificent parent. His love is greater than any earthly parent's love, and His wisdom is greater than any earthly parent's wisdom. God is the perfect parent because He made every person on earth, and He has a plan for each of them.

God puts us in families where He expects moms and dads to teach their children to love and respect Him as their heavenly Father. He expects children to respect their parents here on earth and to grow strong believing in Jesus.

Families grow and change. But God does not change. He will always and forever be your loving heavenly Father.

Memory Verses

· ·

The Bible has many verses about God the Father. Memorize the ones below. Then see if you can find more in your Bible.

For us there is but one God, the Father, from whom all things came and for whom we live; and there is but one Lord, Jesus Christ, through whom all things came and through whom we live.

1 Corinthians 8:6 NIV

· · · · · ·

For his Spirit joins with our spirit to affirm that we are God's children.

Romans 8:16 NLT

· · · · · ·

Father to the fatherless, defender of widows— this is God, whose dwelling is holy.

Psalm 68:5 NLT

One God and Father of all, who is above all, and through all, and in you all.

Ephesians 4:6 KJV

• • • • • •

Fear not, little flock; for it is your Father's good pleasure to give you the kingdom.

Luke 12:32 KJV

• • • • • •

Every good and perfect gift is from above, coming down from the Father of the heavenly lights, who does not change like shifting shadows.

James 1:17 NIV

Memory Plan

· · · · · · · · · · · · · · · · · ·

Jesus taught people how to pray to our heavenly Father. You might know His prayer as the "Lord's Prayer." If you don't know the Lord's Prayer, memorize it now. When you find yourself in a situation where you don't know how to pray, you can always say the Lord's Prayer, and your heavenly Father will hear you.

> Our Father which art in heaven, Hallowed be thy name.
> Thy kingdom come. Thy will be done in earth,
>   as it is in heaven.
> Give us this day our daily bread.
> And forgive us our debts, as we forgive our debtors.
> And lead us not into temptation, but deliver us from evil:
> For thine is the kingdom, and the power, and the glory,
>   for ever. Amen. (Matthew 6:9–13 KJV)

CHAPTER 47

• • • • • • • • • • • • • •

JESUS, GOD'S SON

▶▶ Jesus Is Lord

If God is our heavenly Father, then who is Jesus? He is a part of God. Jesus is God's Son. The Bible says that Jesus is Lord.

That Jesus is Lord means that He is the earth's Great Ruler. He rules over us and shows us how to live a life pleasing to God. Jesus has power over whether or not we will live forever in heaven one day. He is the one and only way to heaven. If you believe that Jesus is Lord, that He died on the cross for your sins and then came back to life, you will live with Him in heaven.

Jesus is the perfect Lord of *you*. He is good, and He loves you so much. He wants you to be like His disciples and follow Him. You do that by learning as much as you can about Him and trying your best to be like Him. You should love Jesus with all your heart and make Him the most important One in your life.

The Lord Jesus is with you all the time. You cannot see Him, but He is there. You can count on Him, not only as Lord, but also as your very best friend.

Memory Verses

· · · · · · · · · · · · · · · · · · · ·

The New Testament is full of the stories and
teachings of Jesus. Here are several Bible verses
to memorize to remind you that Jesus is Lord.

He is Lord of lords, and King of kings: and they that are with
him are called, and chosen, and faithful.

Revelation 17:14 KJV

· · · · · ·

It is written: "'As surely as I live,' says the Lord, 'every knee will
bow before me; every tongue will acknowledge God.'"

Romans 14:11 NIV

· · · · · ·

If you declare with your mouth, "Jesus is Lord," and believe
in your heart that God raised him from the dead, you will be
saved.

Romans 10:9 NIV

For the wages of sin is death, but the free gift of God is eternal life through Christ Jesus our Lord.

Romans 6:23 NLT

• • • • • •

And whatever you do, whether in word or deed, do it all in the name of the Lord Jesus, giving thanks to God the Father through him.

Colossians 3:17 NIV

• • • • • •

And now, just as you accepted Christ Jesus as your Lord, you must continue to follow him.

Colossians 2:6 NLT

Memory Plan

Here is a fun scripture relay race that you and your friends can play in teams: You will need two individual chalkboards and someone who will not play the game but be the leader.

1. Divide into teams.
2. The leader calls out one of the scripture references from this chapter. For example, "Revelation 17:14!"
3. The first player in each team writes the first word of the scripture verse on the chalkboard and then passes the board to the next person.
4. That person writes the second word of the verse and passes the board to the third person.
5. Play continues until the entire verse has been written on that team's board.
6. The first team to finish the verse correctly wins.

You could also play the game as a running relay. Use a big chalkboard and have team members run to the board to write their words.

CHAPTER 48

• • • • • • • • • • • • • •

GOD IS REAL

▶▶ Really Real!

You already know the difference between fiction and nonfiction. Fiction is about something that is made up. Nonfiction is about something that is real.

God is real. Jesus is real. Everything in the Bible is 100 percent true and real. Jesus' disciple Peter wrote: "For we were not making up clever stories when we told you about the powerful coming of our Lord Jesus Christ. We saw his majestic splendor with our own eyes" (2 Peter 1:16 NLT).

Jesus lived on earth as a man. People saw Him, talked with Him, and touched Him. He is just as real as you are! And all the stories Jesus told and all the things He said are true. If ever you find yourself doubting God or the Bible, you can ask Jesus to help you believe.

Jesus said, "Stop doubting" (John 20:27 NIV). Sometimes it is hard to believe because you cannot see God. But Jesus said that by faith you *can* believe that God exists. Why? Because Jesus said so. And Jesus is a part of God, and God cannot lie. Jesus tells the truth—always. So don't doubt. Believe!

Memory Verses

. . . .

The enemy, Satan, wants to trick you into thinking that
God is a made-up god. Memorize these Bible truths,
and don't allow yourself to be tricked.

For we were not making up clever stories when we told you
about the powerful coming of our Lord Jesus Christ. We saw
his majestic splendor with our own eyes.

2 Peter 1:16 NLT

. . . . . .

For ever since the world was created, people have seen the
earth and sky. Through everything God made, they can clearly
see his invisible qualities—his eternal power and divine nature.
So they have no excuse for not knowing God.

Romans 1:20 NLT

. . . . . .

But without faith it is impossible to please him: for he that
cometh to God must believe that he is, and that he is a
rewarder of them that diligently seek him.

Hebrews 11:6 KJV

No one has ever seen God, but the one and only Son, who is himself God and is in closest relationship with the Father, has made him known.

John 1:18 NIV

• • • • • •

When you ask, you must believe and not doubt, because the one who doubts is like a wave of the sea, blown and tossed by the wind.

James 1:6 NIV

• • • • • •

Then he said to Thomas, "Put your finger here; see my hands. Reach out your hand and put it into my side. Stop doubting and believe."

John 20:27 NIV

Memory Plan

· · · · · · · · · · · · · · · · · ·

Play "Truth or Doubt" with a family member or friend. One person reads a memory verse from this chapter and either reads it correctly or changes it in some way. The other person says, "Truth," if the verse is correct, or "Doubt," if it is incorrect.

Try it with other memory verses in this book. How many will you get right?

CHAPTER 49

• • • • • • • • • • • • • • •

APPEARANCE

▶▶ Skin Deep

How do you define "beauty" or "handsomeness"? Do certain celebrities come to mind? Many people define beauty by how a person looks on the outside. But recognizing beauty only by what is skin deep can get you into trouble.

Some women wear beautiful jewelry and clothing, and some men work out and have muscular bodies. There is nothing wrong with looking good and staying in shape. But looks have nothing to do with what a person looks like on the inside.

The Bible says, "The Lord does not look at the things people look at. People look at the outward appearance, but the Lord looks at the heart" (1 Samuel 16:7 NIV). That is how God expects humans to judge beauty in each other—not by how someone looks, but rather by what is inside his or her heart.

You can tell what is in someone's heart by the things they say and how they act. Ask yourself, *Is this person speaking and acting in a way that is pleasing to the Lord?* If the answer is yes, then that person has the best kind of beauty—a beautiful heart.

Remember—outward beauty fades with time, but inner beauty lasts forever.

Memory Verses

• •

Memorize these verses, and remember them
whenever you are tempted to judge someone
by beauty or handsomeness that is skin deep.

"The LORD does not look at the things people look at. People
look at the outward appearance, but the LORD looks at the
heart."

1 Samuel 16:7 NIV

• • • • • •

Your beauty should not come from outward adornment, such
as elaborate hairstyles and the wearing of gold jewelry or
fine clothes. Rather, it should be that of your inner self, the
unfading beauty of a gentle and quiet spirit, which is of great
worth in God's sight.

1 Peter 3:3–4 NIV

• • • • • •

"Physical training is good, but training for godliness is much
better, promising benefits in this life and in the life to come."

1 Timothy 4:8 NLT

Charm is deceptive, and beauty is fleeting; but a woman who fears the LORD is to be praised.

Proverbs 31:30 NIV

. . . . . .

"In the same way, on the outside you appear to people as righteous but on the inside you are full of hypocrisy and wickedness."

Matthew 23:28 NIV

. . . . . .

As the Scriptures say, "People are like grass; their beauty is like a flower in the field. The grass withers and the flower fades. But the word of the Lord remains forever."

1 Peter 1:24–25 NLT

Memory Plan

....

Write each of the verses in this chapter on sticky notes. Put the notes on the bathroom mirror, near your closet, or wherever else you get dressed and ready. As you memorize each verse, think about how you view your own beauty or handsomeness. Are you focused only on your looks, or are you focused on your beautiful heart?

CHAPTER 50

· · · · · · · · · · · · · ·

ANIMALS

▶▶ Do Pets Go to Heaven?

Do pets go to heaven? The Bible doesn't say they will. It doesn't say they won't, either! Whether or not pets go to heaven is one question only God can answer.

We do know that God made animals and they pleased Him. The Bible says, "God made all sorts of wild animals, livestock, and small animals, each able to produce offspring of the same kind. And God saw that it was good" (Genesis 1:25 NLT). And we know that God takes care of animals: "Look at the birds. They don't plant or harvest or store food in barns, for your heavenly Father feeds them" (Matthew 6:26 NLT). It is also a fact that someday God will create a new and perfect earth and animals will be there. "In that day the wolf and the lamb will live together; the leopard will lie down with the baby goat. The calf and the yearling will be safe with the lion, and a little child will lead them all" (Isaiah 11:6 NLT).

Maybe our pets do go to heaven! But for now, it is our job to love them here on earth and trust that God has a perfect plan for them, just as He does for us.

Memory Verses

· · · · · · · · · · · · · · · · · · · ·

Do you have a pet, and sometimes caring for it is a chore?
Memorize these verses to remember that you should
help care for God's animals and do it willingly.

God made all sorts of wild animals, livestock, and small
animals, each able to produce offspring of the same kind. And
God saw that it was good.

Genesis 1:25 NLT

· · · · · ·

He giveth to the beast his food, and to the young ravens which
cry.

Psalm 147:9 KJV

· · · · · ·

Are not five sparrows sold for two pennies? Yet not one of
them is forgotten by God.

Luke 12:6 NIV

"In his hand is the life of every creature and the breath of all mankind."

Job 12:10 NIV

• • • • • •

Then shall the dust return to the earth as it was: and the spirit shall return unto God who gave it.

Ecclesiastes 12:7 KJV

• • • • • •

In that day the wolf and the lamb will live together; the leopard will lie down with the baby goat. The calf and the yearling will be safe with the lion, and a little child will lead them all.

Isaiah 11:6 NLT

Memory Plan

Memorize these verses together with family members or with friends from your church. Then brainstorm ways you can help animals in your community. You could donate food, cat litter, or other supplies to an animal shelter. You might also help at a shelter cleaning cages or other areas. If your family is thinking of getting a pet, adopting from a shelter is a great thing to do. You will be helping an animal and also giving it a forever home. Can you think of other ways to help dogs, cats, and other pets? What about birds and other wild animals where you live?

Think about It

. . . .

Why do you think there are some questions about God and heaven that people can't answer?

Do you think animals are important to God?

Which did God make first, people or animals? Hint: Read the first chapter of Genesis.

You memorized a verse about God's new earth that says: "The wolf and the lamb will live together; the leopard will lie down with the baby goat. The calf and the yearling will be safe with the lion" (Isaiah 11:6 NLT). What do you think that means? Hint: Think about earth today and predators and prey.

Can you name at least five animals that are mentioned in the Bible?

What is your opinion? Do you think animals go to heaven? Why or why not?

CHAPTER 51

· · · · · · · · · · · · · · · ·

LONELINESS

▶▶ You Belong!

Loneliness usually means feeling sad because you are without company. But you can also feel lonely with people around you, like when you are a new kid in a new school on your first day. Loneliness is a sadness that comes from inside of you, a feeling that says, *I don't belong. I don't fit in.*

But you *do* belong, and you *do* fit in! Why? Because God made you to belong in His world. You are so very loved by Him that He is with you always. Never will God leave you alone.

Jesus went through an awful alone time when everyone seemed to hate Him. The Bible says, "He was despised and rejected—a man of sorrows, acquainted with deepest grief. We turned our backs on him and looked the other way. He was despised, and we did not care" (Isaiah 53:3 NLT). What did Jesus do? He turned to His heavenly Father for companionship. He prayed and spent time with God.

Whenever you feel lonely, be like Jesus. Spend time with God. Ask Him to bring good people into your life to keep you company. Then trust Him to do it, and remember—God is with you all the time.

Memory Verses

· · · · · · · · · · · · · · · · · · · ·

These verses are like armor. They will remind you that
God cares. They will protect you from Satan's voice that
whispers, *"You don't belong."* Memorize these promises.
Hold them tight in your heart.

Even if my father and mother abandon me, the LORD will hold
me close.

Psalm 27:10 NLT

· · · · · ·

God sets the lonely in families.

Psalm 68:6 NIV

· · · · · ·

He healeth the broken in heart, and bindeth up their wounds.

Psalm 147:3 KJV

"For the sake of his great name the LORD will not reject his people, because the LORD was pleased to make you his own."

1 Samuel 12:22 NIV

• • • • • •

Come close to God, and God will come close to you.

James 4:8 NLT

• • • • • •

"No one will be able to stand against you as long as you live. For I will be with you as I was with Moses. I will not fail you or abandon you."

Joshua 1:5 NLT

Memory Plan

•••••••••••••••••••

Make a poster collage using photos of your family and friends or pictures that you draw of them. In the middle of the collage put the words *I BELONG!* Then memorize each of the Bible verses in this chapter and write them on your collage. Put the collage in your room where you can see it. Whenever you feel lonely, use the collage to remind you that you are never alone.

CHAPTER 52

. . . .

STILLNESS/NIGHTTIME

▶▶ Be Still

Maybe you know this Bible promise: "Be still, and know that I am God." It comes from Psalm 46:10. When you think of being still, you might think of nighttime because that is when most people rest. Just before bedtime is one of the best times to be still, to think about God, and to spend time with Him.

The Bible has some beautiful things to say about nighttime. It reminds us that when we look up at the night sky, we can only see a little of what is up there. No human knows what is beyond the stars, but God knows, and He is there in "the heights of heaven" (Job 22:12 NIV). And the Bible says that even the moon and stars praise Him (see Psalm 148:3). It reminds us to "consider the heavens" and think of how small we are when compared with God and His creation. Still, as small as we are in comparison to Him, He cares so deeply for us (see Psalm 8:3–4 KJV). The Bible even suggests that we sing our bedtime prayers! (see Psalm 42:8).

Tonight, look up at the sky and have a long talk with God. He is waiting to hear from you.

Memory Verses

. . . .

Memorize these verses. Then repeat them to yourself at bedtime before you say your prayers.

Be still, and know that I am God.

Psalm 46:10 KJV

. . . . . .

"God is so great—higher than the heavens, higher than the farthest stars."

Job 22:12 NLT

. . . . . .

When I consider your heavens, the work of your fingers, the moon and the stars, which you have set in place, what is mankind that you are mindful of them, human beings that you care for them?

Psalm 8:3–4 NIV

But each day the LORD pours his unfailing love upon me, and through each night I sing his songs, praying to God who gives me life.

Psalm 42:8 NLT

• • • • • •

Praise ye him, sun and moon: praise him, all ye stars of light.

Psalm 148:3 KJV

• • • • • •

Then Jesus said, "Come to me, all of you who are weary and carry heavy burdens, and I will give you rest."

Matthew 11:28 NLT

Memory Plan

. . . .

There are more than three hundred memory verses in this book. Did you memorize them all? If you did, good for you! And if you didn't memorize all of them, that's okay, too. You can try again. Ask God to help you to know Him by remembering what He says and holding His words in your heart.

You have worked very hard at memorizing God's words and His promises, so take time to be still. Rest in the Lord, and remember that He loves you. He is with you now, tomorrow—and forever.

Think about It

· · · · · · · · · · · · · · · · · · · ·

Which did you find to be the best way for you to memorize the verses in this book?

What did you learn about memorizing God's Word—the Bible?

Can you come up with your own creative ways to memorize scripture?

If you could meet God right now, what would you say to Him?

If memorizing scripture is difficult for you, whom could you ask to be your scripture memory helper?

Is knowing God's Word a priority in your home? How can you and your family members share learning the Bible together?

Scripture Verses by Topic

FRIENDSHIP
Jeremiah 29:11
Proverbs 22:11
Zephaniah 3:17
Proverbs 17:17
Revelation 3:20
Ecclesiastes 4:9

ALL ABOUT ME
Psalm 139:16
John 1:12
1 Corinthians 6:19
1 Corinthians 6:20
Ephesians 2:10
Psalm 139:14

CHALLENGES
Philippians 4:13
1 Chronicles 28:20
Isaiah 41:13
Psalm 18:32
Deuteronomy 31:6
Joshua 1:9

COURAGE
Joshua 1:7
2 Chronicles 15:7
1 Corinthians 16:13
Psalm 31:24
Isaiah 43:2–3
Ephesians 6:11

PRAYER
Psalm 55:17
Isaiah 30:19
Psalm 145:18
Psalm 91:15
1 Peter 3:12
1 Thessalonians 5:17

FEAR
Isaiah 41:10
2 Timothy 1:7
Proverbs 3:24
Psalm 91:4–5
Isaiah 43:2
Hebrews 13:6

GRACE
Ephesians 4:7
Ephesians 2:8–9
Luke 2:40
2 Corinthians 12:9
Psalm 23:1
Psalm 20:4

FAITH
Hebrews 11:1
1 Samuel 2:9
Romans 3:22
Luke 17:6
James 2:17
Galatians 3:26

PATIENCE
James 1:4
Lamentations 3:25
Isaiah 40:31
Hebrews 10:36
Hebrews 6:12
Romans 8:25

CHILDREN'S DUTIES
Colossians 3:20
Deuteronomy 5:16
Proverbs 6:20
Proverbs 10:1

Proverbs 20:11
Proverbs 23:26

GUILT/GOD'S FORGIVENESS
1 John 2:12
1 John 1:9
1 John 3:20
Jeremiah 31:34
Isaiah 55:7
Hebrews 8:12

FORGIVING OTHERS
Matthew 6:14
Matthew 5:44
Luke 6:35
Ephesians 4:31–32
Matthew 18:21–22
Luke 6:37

TRUST
Proverbs 3:5–6
Psalm 40:4
Psalm 37:5
Psalm 28:7
Jeremiah 17:7–8
Proverbs 29:25

ANGER
Proverbs 29:11
Proverbs 15:1
Colossians 3:8
James 1:19–20
Ephesians 4:26
Psalm 145:8

GOD'S PEACE
Philippians 4:6–7
Psalm 4:8
2 Thessalonians 3:16
1 Corinthians 14:33
Daniel 10:19
John 14:27

PEACE WITH OTHERS
Matthew 5:9
Romans 12:18
Psalm 34:14
Proverbs 3:17
Proverbs 17:1
James 3:18

JUDGING OTHERS
Matthew 7:1–2
Matthew 7:3
Matthew 7:4
John 7:24
John 8:7
James 4:12

THE WORLD
John 3:16
1 John 4:4
Psalm 24:1
John 3:17
Psalm 96:13
John 16:33

GOD'S LOVE FOR US
Romans 5:8
1 John 4:16
1 John 3:1

Psalm 103:11
Romans 8:39
Psalm 136:1

WORSHIP/ LOVING GOD
Psalm 100:2
Deuteronomy 6:5
Psalm 95:6
Nehemiah 9:6
Psalm 29:2
Luke 4:8

LOVING OTHERS
John 15:12
1 Corinthians 13:4–5
1 Corinthians 13:5
1 Corinthians 13:6
1 Corinthians 13:7
1 John 3:18

SPEECH/WORDS
Exodus 20:7
Ephesians 5:4
Ephesians 4:29
Proverbs 21:23
Matthew 12:36
Psalm 19:14

GOSSIP
Proverbs 11:13
Proverbs 16:28
Proverbs 20:19
Proverbs 26:20
Proverbs 18:8
Proverbs 20:19

LYING
Proverbs 12:22
Numbers 23:19
Exodus 20:16
Colossians 3:9
Psalm 120:2
John 8:44

PRIDE
Proverbs 16:18
Proverbs 29:23
Psalm 138:6
Galatians 6:3
Jeremiah 9:23
Proverbs 26:12

HUMILITY
Philippians 2:3–4
1 Peter 5:5
1 Peter 5:6
Psalm 25:9
Matthew 5:5
1 Peter 3:8

GUIDANCE
John 14:6
Isaiah 30:21
Psalm 48:14
Psalm 37:23
Psalm 143:8
John 10:27

OBEDIENCE
Exodus 19:5
Jeremiah 7:23
James 1:22
James 1:23–24
1 John 2:3
1 John 2:5

THE BIBLE

Revelation 21:5
2 Timothy 3:16
John 1:1
Isaiah 40:8
Romans 15:4
Matthew 24:35

WISDOM

James 1:5
Proverbs 4:11–12
1 Corinthians 1:25
James 3:17
Proverbs 3:7
Proverbs 3:13

FRUITFULNESS

Galatians 5:22–23
John 15:8
Luke 6:43
Luke 6:44
Matthew 7:20
Psalm 1:2–3

TEMPTATION

Matthew 4:10
Matthew 6:13
1 Corinthians 10:13
Matthew 26:41
James 4:7
James 1:12

MONEY

Matthew 19:21
Matthew 6:24
Hebrews 13:5
1 Timothy 6:10
Matthew 6:21
Proverbs 3:9

ETERNAL LIFE

1 John 2:25
John 11:25
John 11:26
John 14:2–3
John 17:3
1 Thessalonians 4:14

THE HOLY SPIRIT

John 14:16
John 14:18
John 14:26
Romans 8:26
Romans 5:5
Galatians 5:16

JOY!

Philippians 4:4
Psalm 118:24
Psalm 28:7
Psalm 67:4
Romans 12:12
Ecclesiastes 11:9

HOPE

Psalm 39:7
Job 11:18
Psalm 25:5
Psalm 42:5
Lamentations 3:25
Micah 7:7

PERSEVERANCE

Galatians 6:9
1 Corinthians 15:58
1 Corinthians 9:24
Ecclesiastes 7:8
2 Timothy 4:7
2 Corinthians 8:11

CHILDREN

Psalm 127:3
2 Timothy 3:14
Psalm 8:2
Matthew 18:3
Mark 9:36–37
Proverbs 22:6

WORRY/ANXIETY

Philippians 4:6
Matthew 6:26
Matthew 6:27
Matthew 6:30
1 Peter 5:7
Proverbs 12:25

PRIORITIES

Matthew 22:37
Exodus 20:3
Matthew 6:33
John 15:5
John 3:30
Revelation 22:13

STRENGTH

Ephesians 3:16
Isaiah 40:29
Habakkuk 3:19
Psalm 46:1
2 Samuel 22:33
Ephesians 6:10

LAZINESS

Proverbs 6:6
Proverbs 6:10–11
Proverbs 13:4
Proverbs 28:19
Proverbs 12:24
Romans 12:11

MERCY

Psalm 86:5
Luke 6:36
1 Peter 1:3
Hebrews 4:16
Psalm 145:9
Psalm 23:6

CHARITY

Luke 6:38
Psalm 41:1
1 Corinthians 13:13
2 Corinthians 9:7
Matthew 5:42
Matthew 25:35

GOD THE FATHER

1 Corinthians 8:6
Romans 8:16
Psalm 68:5
Ephesians 4:6
Luke 12:32
James 1:17

JESUS, GOD'S SON

Revelation 17:14
Romans 14:11
Romans 10:9
Romans 6:23
Colossians 3:17
Colossians 2:6

GOD IS REAL

2 Peter 1:16
Romans 1:20
Hebrews 11:6
John 1:18
James 1:6
John 20:27

APPEARANCE

1 Samuel 16:7
1 Peter 3:3–4
1 Timothy 4:8
Proverbs 31:30
Matthew 23:28
1 Peter 1:24–25

ANIMALS

Genesis 1:25
Psalm 147:9
Luke 12:6
Job 12:10
Ecclesiastes 12:7
Isaiah 11:6

LONELINESS

Psalm 27:10
Psalm 68:6
Psalm 147:3
1 Samuel 12:22
James 4:8
Joshua 1:5

STILLNESS/ NIGHTTIME

Psalm 46:10
Job 22:12
Psalm 8:3–4
Psalm 42:8
Psalm 148:3
Matthew 11:28